Ghost Hunting

A Beginners Guide to Investigating the Dead

(The Essential Modern Guide to Ghost Hunting for Beginners)

James Trainor

Published By **Oliver Leish**

James Trainor

All Rights Reserved

Ghost Hunting: A Beginners Guide to Investigating the Dead (The Essential Modern Guide to Ghost Hunting for Beginners)

ISBN 978-1-7779885-2-4

No part of this guidebook shall be reproduced in any form without permission in writing from the publisher except in the case of brief quotations embodied in critical articles or reviews.

Legal & Disclaimer

The information contained in this book is not designed to replace or take the place of any form of medicine or professional medical advice. The information in this book has been provided for educational & entertainment purposes only.

The information contained in this book has been compiled from sources deemed reliable, and it is accurate to the best of the Author's knowledge; however, the Author cannot guarantee its accuracy and validity and cannot be held liable for any errors or omissions. Changes are periodically made to this book. You must consult your doctor or get professional medical advice before using any of the suggested remedies, techniques, or information in this book.

Upon using the information contained in this book, you agree to hold harmless the Author from and against any damages, costs, and expenses, including any legal fees potentially resulting from the application of any of the information provided by this guide. This disclaimer applies to any damages or injury caused by the use and application, whether directly or indirectly, of any advice or information presented, whether for breach of contract, tort, negligence, personal injury, criminal intent, or under any other cause of action.

You agree to accept all risks of using the information presented inside this book. You need to consult a professional medical practitioner in order to ensure you are both able and healthy enough to participate in this program.

Table Of Contents

Chapter 1: The Truth About Ghost Studies Revealed 1

Chapter 2: What Happens If We Are Stressed? 9

Chapter 3: How To Go Ghost Hunting 20

Chapter 4: The Appeal Of Ghost Hunting Is Increasing 30

Chapter 5: Enhance Your Safety On Ghost Hunts 38

Chapter 6: What Happens During A Ghost Hunt? 48

Chapter 7: What Are Ghosts And Why Do We Hunt Them? 60

Chapter 8: What Tools Will I Need? 68

Chapter 9: My Favorite Ghost Hunting Techniques............................. 77

Chapter 10: Putting Together Your Ghost Hunting Team 84

- Chapter 11: Conducting Your First Ghost Hunt 90
- Chapter 12: Torches Lighting 101
- Chapter 13: Evp Equipment 108
- Chapter 14: The Efp Stands For Evp Field Processor 114
- Chapter 15: Franks Box 126
- Chapter 16: Shadow Detector 134
- Chapter 17: What Qualities Are Exhibited By Ghost Hunters? 145
- Chapter 18: Keeping Accurate Records 153
- Chapter 19: Building And Organizing A Team 164
- Chapter 20: Follow Strict Protocols To Protect Credibility 174
- Chapter 21: Instinct Versus Intellect 181

Chapter 1: The Truth About Ghost Studies Revealed

Since the beginning of time, both people who believe and those who don't have faith are intrigued by ghosts. They've provided us with plenty of ideas to talk about, films and stories, poetry or songs, books as well as other items. There is a debate about ghosts' existence remains just as heated like it was a few years earlier. The majority of the population believes in ghosts. The remaining half are rationalists who think that science has the ability to be the cause of everything that happens on Earth.

Definition of Ghost A ghost (or spirit) of a dead person who is unable to let go of the physical plane to enter the higher realms is usually referred to"ghost. "ghost." In the case of strong attraction to particular people, locations items, objects or an not being finished with work, the spirit could have resisted leaving. In the case of a murder, for instance, a victim could stay until the execution of his attacker. Ghosts can also be thought of as being demons or other spirits of the astral realm.

The majority of the time there is a belief ghosts are haunting old houses or graveyards, locations that people have died or even places that were crucial to them.

Hauntings, spirits communication as well as apparitions, ghosts, and many other paranormal events have been documented meticulously over the course of hundreds of years.

It's not easy to research ghosts. Ghosts are rarely disruptive to the life of living people and tend to remain in their own world. To investigate an incident that has occurred, you're not able to summon ghosts on your own.

But, certain spirits could be able to come out and contribute to the investigation. For instance you won't be able to spot a ghost or speak to it until the spirit will talk with you.

Techniques to Research Ghosts Technology has created a variety of tools which make it simpler to research ghosts. Digital voice recorders, infrared sensor thermal cameras, Geiger counters are all used by ghost hunters in order to find evidence to prove the ghosts' existence. Paranormal researchers greatly profit from the information gathered by these devices.

Ghosts however are able to be studied by mediums of spirit without the aid of technological devices or technology. They possess the sixth sense, which can allow them to sense what the ordinary human being cannot. They also can perceive the supernatural. Even though science can't determine if the experiences of a medium are true or not, mediums can significantly aid in studies on the supernatural.

Through the use of the science and logic With the aid of logic and science, it's impossible to establish that ghosts do exist. Although ghosts have been investigated over the years, there is not enough evidence to prove the existence of ghosts. Similar to how believers are armed with plenty of evidence that supports their assertions, those who are not believers are able to provide a wealth of tales that support their argument. At the end of the day, all of it is determined by your personal beliefs and experience.

Haunted Happenings is an original ghost hunting service.

Ghost Hunting The Art of a Successful Ghost Hunt Event

It is our goal to engage our guests to create a memorable experience of ghost hunting at every event. Participants are part of the research and work with the paranormal group. In vigils, they are taught how to be in control and let their feelings dictate their actions. They are respectful of the distinctiveness of every ghost hunt. Through the course of the hunt every guest is made conscious of any ghost or ghostly activity that is occurring in the vicinity. In the course of the actual hunt, guests can share their discoveries with paranormal investigators while they conduct investigations using equipment for ghost hunting.

An effective ghost hunt will not necessarily happen with a large amount of activities since, despite the fact that it is a frightening experience and exactly what the people are looking for but it is not easily understood because the hunt is not structured or supported. Therefore, individuals might be in a state in a state of confusion about what they have observed or heard if the information is not discussed or set in context with the format of a ghost hunt. It is my understanding that some people might want to hold the seances and vigils themselves with no interference from others. It is possible that they are not prepared for the events that could occur when they are on their own according to my experience. Being part of the group It is essential to provide your guests with an impression that they're doing their own rituals However, in actual we monitor them closely and monitor the way they feel after their sole time vigil.

In the end, I'd consider that a successful hunt isn't so all about the things that happen in a supernatural way, but it's about how much passion and excitement is kept even when there is no activity. Ghost Hunting - What Actually Happens? This is that we need to make the maximum effort to preserve the visitors "spirits."

What are the real actions and results of a ghost hunting?

The majority of haunted places are frequented by people hoping that they'll see signs of something supernatural. In most cases, the host will give an introduction before taking the guests through a historical excursion of the area in the course of a haunted hunt. There are two advantages to this one is that you know a bit more about the history of the region and sightings reported, and in addition, you'll get an opportunity to establish your orientation and familiarize yourself with the location you'll spend your evening.

Following that, you'll have be allowed the opportunity to go in search of ghosts independently with your own vigils. Following that, you'll need to meet with your medium for the duration of the evening. They should be able to talk about ghosts and spirits that they feel around them during that time.

Then, you'll be divided into smaller groups, and then asked to engage in various activities and vigils designed in order to determine if you are able to cause anything supernatural to happen.

Chapter 2: What Happens If We Are Stressed?

There's no reason to be criticized or scolded about being afraid as will anyone else. I'm confident in telling that, although I'm a seasoned ghost hunter, there's a time while on a hunt and I'm caught by the surprise of. What I can offer is that you must persevere, since the rewards of conquering the fear of being afraid is a gift from the realm of spirits. But, be assured that you're in safe in our hands, and we'll help you out should you do get too much.

Do you know of costumed characters who come out of the dark?

It's very unlikely that a group or group of people could even be considered being a paranormal group or even charge for events that are advertised as authentic ghost hunts in the event that they employ actors who would fabricate witnesses in the course of the hunt. We are convinced that any of these incidents is real However, I've gone to a cold castle in the early hours of 3 a.m. but there has been no evidence of anything happening. This is the chance you're taking. All it takes is one event to occur to you, and you'll become in love, I assure you.

What do I need for to conduct the ghost hunt?

Make sure you wear something warm as certain places where you're likely to visit do not provide heating, windows or fires. Or anything other than that. So, bring plenty of layers in order to remove them when you're excessively hot. Wear comfortable, sensible shoes or sneakers. If your location is outside it is recommended to wear waterproofs. They are extremely useful. An emergency torch when wandering around at night as well as a camera camcorder, as well as any other medications that you normally take, such as asthma medication. Ghost hunting takes an extended time, and requires lots of patience however, it is usually rewarding whenever something occurs that leaves you wondering about ghosts or spirits.

The Basics of Ghost Hunting

The distinction between the two types of investigation is the very first step to mastering the basics of ghost hunts. The terms ghost hunt and investigation aren't always exactly the same. When someone does a ghost hunt you are searching for the signs of spirits or ghosts at places that nobody has seen the ghosts. Ghost investigations involve traveling to an area which is believed to be haunted, and then taking notes that can be later reviewed.

If you're searching for ghosts or investigating the subject, it is important to make use of audio and video recording equipment to gather proof. It is also advisable to conduct research about the history of the area and also conduct interviews with individuals interested, taking notes throughout the process. There is a chance that you'll be trying to eliminate the spirits when you look into the possibility of a haunting. Even if you do not feel like stopping the ghosts, you may have the ability to bring the proprietor of the house to contact somebody who's been there before.

It is important to bear on your toes that there are numerous types of spirits to consider when searching at or researching ghosts. There are many reasons why some spirits are just ghosts of people who died and remain present. Beings that never were humans are called other spirits. The most common "ghost" are dead people. They may be swarming around areas for any number of motives, such as in the case of unsolved issues or refusing to accept their death. This type of spirit most likely poses a threat. Don't approach anyone of the spirit without being prepared. In the case of investigating an incident one should think about the possibility of seeing an un-human entity in your mind despite the fact that such sightings are not common.

A Basic Guideline to Beginning Ghost Hunters Because things aren't always like they do in the darkness You must spend your time in the area you'll be investigating at all times of the day.

If you're in the in the middle of a field, or in an old cemetery It's possible that you don't think that it's necessary at the moment however, it is essential to obtain permission prior to looking for ghosts in private properties. Apart from being unlawful the act of trespassing is a risk to.

If you're required to show proof of identity, you need that you have this document. What authorization did you get? While you are investigating, take an original with you in order to prove you're not in violation.

Do not conduct a search independently. As you're likely searching for ghosts and you could be injured or even killed, and you do not need to feel alone in the event that anything bad happens.

If possible, you should schedule your explorations and hunts to in the evening. However, be sure to snap photographs and video during your day, too.

Do your homework. Newspapers, the internet as well as historical records and interviews with locals provide ideas for places to search for ghosts or ghost stories.

My method for hunting Ghosts My approach to hunt ghosts and paranormal activity is simple and available for almost everyone.

Before you begin, make sure you've got all the equipment that you require to conduct an investigation in a professional manner. The following are among them items: a digital still camera and a night-vision camcorder as well as a temperature gauge most likely one equipped with lasers and an EVP recorder and walkie-talkies should you are separated from the group.

To conduct your initial formal investigation, it is necessary to do some research after you've got the tools. Once you've completed the first step, it's appropriate to go out at times during the day, so you are able to perform an inspection and gain familiar with the place in a calmer time. There is a chance of injuring yourself in the event that you just begin looking around without making a formal investigation for example, within a demolished building.

The next step is to find persons who have been there and experienced experiences there. If more than a handful of witnesses have reported, seen or witnessed something happen in the area, it's definitely to be haunted. Be sure to capture each report in order that, when you go through the film it will be possible to determine whether anything is in line with what interviewees said.

Then you will be able to explore the site. Each site must be equipped with a base. If you're conducting an investigation outdoors in the outdoors, it is important to make a plan for a place to go in the event that you are ever isolated from the group. In open areas It can be difficult to determine where you are during the night. So, it is essential to be aware of this.

EVPs are the kind of evidence said to be found the most. It is because of the fact that ghosts is not requiring as much effort to communicate like it would to show up like an image. Make sure there's an interval of 15 to 30 seconds interval between the inquiries to ghosts in order to get the EVPs. Because ghosts' attempts to communicate require lots of energy.

Learn to Stalk Ghosts!

I am a professional ghost hunter and a lover of spirits, so I am grateful to you for taking the time to read my blog. Although I'm not claiming that I can give you all the information however, I would like to show the basic steps paranormal investigators take in conducting an investigation, and the things they are doing each day.

Step 1: If the proprietor of the company contact you, take their suggestions to get all the background information you can regarding the location or people who resided within it in past times. Understanding how they passed away as well as whether they suffered from an unsavory past can aid in determining the type of person they have. This can be challenging sometimes, but most of the time I'm not sure what to expect and I just guess.

2. During the time of the day, go to the area to check for physical hazards like gaps in the flooring or nails hanging out in the dark, you can mark them using glow-in-thedark tape. Don't alter the house in any way adding, for example, a structure into it for personal purposes. Also, you should set up any devices, such as wiring which would be easier to install at night.

Step 3: Get together with other ghost hunters to discuss the activities they'll be taking part in and how they'll work using their gear. Step 4: Pick the leader. If you're in a group of many it might be beneficial to divide it into smaller groups. Give each group an individual leader. It is possible to do a few jumping jacks and praying or something else that you find helpful in this situation. Personally, the one that I do is to breathe deeply and then say "Here we go!"

Step 5: Walk around the property to gain a feel of spirits. Visit different rooms within the home to discover which areas are haunted by spirits. It is here that experiences and intuition shine.

Step 6: Head out with your tools and notebook. Then, you can instruct the team to start working. Record your thoughts as well as your readings, photos, and pictures and your thoughts or images that you may have seen in your house.

Chapter 3: How To Go Ghost Hunting

On Your Personal Ghost hunt, also known as investigating the paranormal is a exciting, thrilling fun activity. The younger generation is becoming more keen on forming groups of their own investigating paranormal phenomena as well as going on ghost hunting because from the rising interest in paranormal shows on television publications, books, and other shows. But, a lot individuals are fully aware of the basics of ghost searching. If you keep reading I'll guide you through every stage of the ghost hunting procedure.

In the beginning, you require a group, a collection that is willing to look into paranormal activities along with you. To ensure yourself and others ensure that you have competent adult supervision. Start working immediately after you've got an entire group of people.

Locate a location that is haunted now is the time to locate the location that has been haunted. It is possible to search for areas that are open to the public, abandoned buildings and "clients" who think their houses are haunted. Avoid investigating graveyards; it's pointless and inconsiderate, as burial sites should not be occupied by a crowd of ghost hunters with cameras. There are many ways to find local legends or rumors of supernatural activities, create the website in order to attract many more visitors to it or even promote your business in local newspapers using classified ads. It is likely that you'll locate something that is haunting the area you live in.

Get the equipment you need for ghost hunting Prior to beginning an investigation, you'll need a few tools for ghost searching. It is recommended to purchase notebooks, both electronic and paper-based, digital camera, recorders for digital flashlights, camcorders but most important of all batteries since the paranormal can cause batteries to lose battery power very fast. Don't be starving yourself throughout your research, therefore ensure you have drinking water and food as well.

Conduct the necessary research prior to starting your research Also, do some the historical research. Know all possible about the area you're planning to visit such as its history as well as technical details, locals as well as other details. It can greatly aid you with the research process.

Take notes in the field After you've reached the location of paranormal activity You can start recording information. If witnesses are present that you can talk to them, snap a few photos take videos, capture images as well as

EVPs Start an overnight study, and then try to collect as much information as you are able to. If you believe you've witnessed something that's supernatural Try to recreate it If you are able to the possibility is high that it's not.

Aid others if you're experiencing a ghostly experience help others. Being a hunter for ghosts You should also assist individuals who are experiencing supernatural events So, you could seek out psychics or occultists to assist you in dealing to the ghosts that have been chasing you around the neighborhood.

Guidelines for post-investigation time Following your return from investigation, you should examine all the evidence take a look at all the images and listen to all the recorded conversations, and view each of the videos. Additionally, go through your personal notes. Find anything unusual. the norm, because it may indicate a genuine paranormal activity occurring at the spot you've just been to.

Restart the process when your investigation is complete then you are able to start the process again for an alternative haunting, and conduct a new research. It is possible to be a ghost hunter taking this approach.

The Top 10 Things You Should Never Do While Hunting Ghosts

Thank you for taking the time to read my piece. Because I've been an investigator in paranormal investigations and as a ghost hunter for quite a few of years, I'd want to inform you of the top ten mistakes you must not make when conducting your investigation.

10. Don't violate any rules: I've learned by personal experience that as a child respecting the rules can help you earn the trust and respect from the local

community. Furthermore, it keeps your from being in jail or having to pay huge penalties. Make sure you check whether the property is owned by anyone before you leave, and in the event that they are, seek permission from the property owner. Don't ever break in.

9. Do not litter, especially if you own the property. Respecting not just the property of a particular person but the property of spirits is a way to show respect. Take care to clean up any chalk or electrical wire items you've put in the trash and make sure you clean up the area in the same condition as it was. If you're causing a stir in the community, they may not be happy to continue going about your business as.

8. Do not go to a location on your own could cause more danger as compared to going together. It's crucial for someone to be nearby in case you need who can call for assistance in case of a slip from a shaky

floor or another injury. Even if they do not investigate ghosts.

7. Avoid visiting a place during the night. First Make sure you visit an area during the day to examine the structure and to ensure it's safe. Note any areas that could be hazardous like flooring that is weak, holes or nails protruding out. Be careful with the glow-in-the-dark tape. In addition, having all your equipment up throughout the day makes this process much easier.

6. Do not wear perfumes or colognes as strong scents may cover up the unusual scents that come from spirits. Shower before going out to an investigation, and don't wear shampoos that have strong odors.

5. Be sure to not miss any important information. While conducting my investigation, I keep a list of things which I

make a note of in order to save it, then print. It is also possible to add certain things to my list of items to help with a specific investigation. You should go through everything over and over again to be sure you've got everything. Failing to take this step could delay your investigation, and could cause you to overlook something vital.

4. There is no way to have enough tapes or batteries therefore, always keep backups available. If you plan to do many ghost hunts, suggest searching for them through eBay or at a wholesale market as well as purchasing large quantities of them. My backup stands on my top list, and it only houses batteries as well as tapes.

3. Do not enter any place that you're not at ease. If the place you are in is an area that is not safe, or the building doesn't appear to be capable of handling your weight or else causes you to feel

uncomfortable, follow your instincts and leave the area. Although having to deal with uncomfortable situations is part of the task, everybody has different tolerances. Don't be influenced by peer pressure in the choices you make!

2. There is a chance that you could be misinterpreted as someone who's in violation of the law, drug addict an alcoholic, a prostitute, or simply dangerous. Be sure to carry proof of identity. There is a chance that you will end being questioned by the police without an identification card and evidence to prove of your status as an investigator in the paranormal field. This is still a waste of time even if they eventually know what you're doing. This is another instance where I have the personal experience of my own.

1. Be sure to tell people the location you're in. If you're planning to go to go on

a hunting trip, inform at least one person where you're located and the time you'll be there. Inform as numerous people as you possibly are able to.

Chapter 4: The Appeal Of Ghost Hunting Is Increasing

Not exclusively and not only in not just in the United States but around the around the world too. World-wide viewers appear to be gaining engaged as new paranormal TV shows are aired. In addition, they're taking part at a rapid amount. Ghost hunting appears to be the future for novices and veterans. Are you surprised?

The practice of ghost hunting also referred to as paranormal investigations, can be thrilling, exciting and challenging. Imagine recording the mysterious sight or specter and then sharing the footage with everyone around the globe. However, it can also be dangerous. There is danger in itself of examining a spot in the dark, with very little or no lighting or in a dark area. So, it's best to be prepared.

Knowing the professional, ethical as well as legal and safety issues is a crucial aspect of any paranormal investigation. It should be integrated into every one. Be aware that you don't wish to become the ghost hunter, but rather you're looking to be secure.

Plan for any unexpected situations. In every situation, you should carry the necessary emergency items such as a flashlight or first aid kit cellphone, water bottle and batteries. Also, it's a good idea to pack extra clothing. Your personal safety, and the safety of all members who is on your team is essential. That's correct, group.

Ghost hunting shouldn't be undertaken on its own. The numbers are an important source of security. I would recommend at least three members on the team, with the team leader serving as the third If it is possible. Look for people who are just as passionate as you are with the same goal and ethics when recruiting team members.

When conducting investigations, assign every team member a distinct assignment and make sure you know exactly where they are in all times. Make sure you are organized and, most of all, efficient with your work. A key aspect to consider when ghost hunting is to have a good dedication to your work.

It is crucial to adhere to an ethical code since there is a chance to find evidence every time you conduct an investigation. Be aware that you require authorization to return to the site to conduct further investigation. Return the website to the original state. Do not alter the website in any way, or demolish the site or any portion of it.

The future investigation of the owner of the site are greatly benefited by polite conduct. Maintain a professional attitude at all times and we'll get back to legal matters.

Investigators are often unaware of the legal aspects. Although most don't even think about the issue, it's essential to consider. Inform the authorities of the area you live in, say, for example, if are in the process of visiting an area with a burial ground. This is not a problem. Prior to beginning your investigation give them complete and detailed written explanation of your plans. If you are able to attract the attention of neighbors who observe you and your group on the grounds at dark, this information can be useful in case they want to call. The ghost hunt will not be stopped by authorities who send cars to look into the matter. Everyone is thrilled. Do not compromise the team's credibility. After the investigation is over be professional.

Do not be rude after an inquiry. Be sure to thank the customer as well as team members. Make sure to use any information or evidence you gather during the course of an investigation to follow up. Provide it to the client with a professionally designed and crafted package and save a copy to yourself and your team to keep in your archives.

If you maintain the highest standards of professional conduct ethical conduct, morality, and safety, going ghost hunting is a fun and enjoyable pastime for everyone. Enjoy your hunt.

The Dangers of Ghost Hunting

You're considering being a ghost hunter as the men on TV aren't you? You're welcome to put your thoughts in a moment since TV shows don't discuss the risks that investigators from the paranormal are faced with on every instance. When you make the decision to become an investigator This article is intended to inform you of the facts since there are a lot of risks.

Sincerely, I'm certainly not speaking of individuals that might cause harm to the person you are. It's about serious physical dangers. In the case of a particular instance, you could receive a call regarding a matter which isn't truly paranormal as such, but it is the presence of a person who has witnessed supernatural events with a severe mental disease. It is possible that the person who is threatening to attack you. It is also possible to visit an abandoned house thought to be haunted, and then get attacked by drug addicts, thugs homeless individuals, various other criminals. Perhaps robbers created a trap due to the fact that they know they'll have expensive equipment for an investigator in the paranormal field.

Other items, such as rotten wood flooring that can break beneath the body, and they are a common sight within older structures. In addition, if conducting an investigation of the private land, then you could run the chance of being detained by the police, or even being assaulted by wild animal.

Then take into consideration your chances of meeting an unidentified or one that's capable of hurling you down steps, or the possibility of encountering a poltergeist that is extremely violent. How can you get rid of the demon? How do you handle negs? The world is populated with beings that are extremely capable and possess many powers. It is not a good idea to turn down using some of the protective rituals or amulets your trusted psychic could advise you to use.

What should you do to deal with every threat? Do not walk on your own This is a standard. Bring someone along if you're planning to research some thing. If you're part of an investigation team for ghosts make sure you work with a team; don't ever go out on a hunt alone; always bring somebody along. Although this won't protect your from being assaulted or injured, it will add more evidence to your research.

Chapter 5: Enhance Your Safety On Ghost Hunts

Many people have taken into ghost hunting as an interest. If you do take a look at it then you could be wondering whether they're actually safe. You might like to explore when you're fascinated by the supernatural and obscure. The importance of prudence cannot be overstated. Prior to embarking on the hunt for ghosts, think about these safety guidelines.

It's Safety in Numbers It's not an appropriate idea to head alone for a look at something bizarre or possibly mysteriously haunted. A larger number of people is better. When you have a good number of people attending the gathering It will not only become more entertaining however, who wouldn't love someone to verify the paranormal stories you've heard about If you already have an account?

Make yourself ready for emergencies You should carry emergency provisions to your location. Uncharted terrain poses risk because ninety percent of ghost hunts happen during the night, and often in dark. Be sure to carry an emergency kit with first aid and snacks, as well as water as well as a flashlight to carry. Be dressed appropriately for the occasion as well as the season. Consider bringing your own nap bag for such an occasion. It is your choice to use your hands but need to carry some items for security and for the event of an injury.

Learn the most you can about your area's historical past, you'll increase your odds for a successful haunted hunt. There are groups that take paranormal excursions to places that are well-known for where there have been sightings during the previous time. If you study a particular location it is possible to go there where it is likely that you will see or feel some thing, and knowing the location and where it is, you are able to go there safely knowing of possible dangers, and/or knowing it is safe to go in the area.

Begin with organized ghost Hunts Participating in an organized ghost hunt is an excellent method to get a glimpse of the supernatural. Professional mediums regularly conduct ghost hunts. It is possible that you have watched some on TV. The best experience is an organized ghost hunt tour, a seance that lasts all night or some other event led by an experienced ghost hunter, and held at a place where there is a tradition of ghostly sightings.

Got Ghosts?

There is a constant search for evidence that can prove or deny ghosts' existence given the current hype about the afterlife and ghosts. Simply put, there's absolutely no proof. It is not proven regardless of the number of television programs like Ghost Hunters, Ghost Adventures and Paranormal State, to name just a handful. The idea that the evidence presented suggests that we're in the presence of spirits is a major leap in logic. It is founded on faith as neither technology nor more advanced education level can prove whether ghosts are real or not.

In conclusion I am convinced spirits exist all around us. In simple terms, the existence of spirits comes down to faith. That is what we're in this place to nurture. Each human being, kid and even animal that's been on the planet exists today. The only thing that stops us from being able to see these creatures. A veil that allows us to develop in this faith. Then we could be able to see the spirits of God everywhere should this veil be lifted.

Sometimes, the veil becomes thin and it is possible to look into the world of spirits. This is why we believe that ghosts exist and the existence of ghostly incidents.

Concerning the types of spirits you could meet while out exploring. It is important to understand that the spiritual existence predates the existence of all matter. So, the existence of spirits is within animals, human beings or trees. They even exist in the earth.

It is possible to meet spirits of animals or animal while out hunting. There are also those of individuals who've lived their lives and looking for answers to why they died. They're just individuals that share your beliefs and goals. They can be good individuals who have tried to achieve the right thing or are just terrible people. What they do in their spirit world is exactly the same as their attitudes they have in their lives. Be it good or bad, they're.

Demons are an additional kind of spirit is important to understand.

It is important to understand that there aren't nearly as numerous kinds of entities that you imagine there are in the different kinds of groups. Nature spirits, as well as any other names you'd like to assign these are actually beings. The third group of spirits of heaven that revolted and were thrown out of heaven together with Lucifer are the spirits. They were not permitted to come into this world and have a body the way us because they could not maintain their original property. Our sisters and brothers who comprise three-quarters of the children of God have resisted God's plans for us all. They're following Lucifer who is a godly son just like us, and are working to get us down to the levels of suffering through deceit and deceit. People will tell you that you'll know if there is a demon around, due to their smell or manner in which they attack. True, but remember that the Legions of Lucifer can disguise them by claiming to be Light Angels and deceive us.

There are a few popular television shows with ghosts or the supernatural include How Real Are These Ghost Hunters, Paranormal State, Most Haunted as well as Psychic Kids. Are these shows authentic? Do they accurately portray ghostly happenings? Are they authentic paranormal documentaries or was it just to have fun? In truth, it's difficult to determine the answer to any of these queries.

Also, I investigate paranormal phenomena. "Hunting ghosts" is one of many kinds of paranormal activities which I research. We admit that our group occasionally employs psychics and that I employ many of the equipment. So, generally speaking I'm familiar with the paranormal investigation and its position. So, I consider that I have enough knowledge to speak about the truth behind the controversial television programs.

In the beginning, in order to make it clear we must say that none of the programs listed above are designed to be a real investigation. The show I like the most can be described as British Most Haunted because it isn't pretending to explore the supernatural. Period. This is merely a show intended for entertainment. The actors go to haunted places to film their show then leave the location without evidence. Due to this, I enjoy the idea.

In all honesty, it is true that other characters such as Ghost Hunters and Paranormal State utilize real technology as well as a variety of authentic method of research. But, they also sometimes employing strategies that can't be considered genuine and are only for entertainment. In addition, it's strange that whenever the characters in these shows conduct investigations, they usually come across something atypical.

It's much harder to experience paranormal phenomena in the real world. Nearly all incidents are either fakes or errors that are logically explicable. But, every one of the mentioned shows has proof of a remarkable activity. It could be that the situation encompasses everything, and the teams often utilize specific effects.

My theory is simple. These could have been legitimate TV shows. Then the ratings began dropping. The show's producer added"Either you'll create details to increase our ratings, or we'll put this show on hold. It's the way great TV programs are produced today solely to make money. Furthermore, it's unfortunate that it portrays real investigations negative.

Chapter 6: What Happens During A Ghost Hunt?

The need for this unique adventure has been growing despite the incredible growth in interest in ghost hunting in recent times. Although Most Haunted hasn't been on television since the year 2010, viewers all over the world are still enthralled and captivated by shows such as Ghost Hunters and Ghost Adventures.

A lot of people aren't aware of ghost hunting, regardless of their popularity. If you've planned one, the excitement of not knowing exactly what to do can often be overwhelming for people to bear.

It is of paramount significance that the event can accommodate participants with different experiences and provides people who participate in a haunted hunt in the first place, the chance to express their opinions and to ask questions. Workshops are frequently provided to allow people to try Dowsing and discover how to feel emotions. The tools that are employed for the night will be explained in detail so that, when the Vigils begin, you will be able to start right away and make the most value from the time.

Although "investigation teams" sometimes complain they are unable to find evidence if there are more than a handful of people is present, ghost-experience night are usually not a matter of the issue of. The events focus on ordinary individuals having the opportunity to experience something supernatural within a secure, controlled setting in some of the most fascinating (and scary) spots rather than attempting to catch a ghost's appearance on film or take a video of an unreliable EVP (electronic voice phenomenon).

There should be the ability take part in various kinds of activities during your ghost hunt. The most popular among them include Vigils as well as Seances with Ouija Boards, Table Tipping as well as glass Divination. The pure "watch & wait" vigils with no light source in which participants are urged to utilize your senses are very thrilling. The whole experience is likely to make you feel elated and enthralled.

Based on your own personal experience, integrity is the top quality you should look at in any business. It's better to leave an area without having had a personal experience and knowing the experience was authentic than go home wondering if it was fake. The winner is when your team has a clear and honest approach to the event. announces it in their first announcements.

The law should permit you to make use of the paranormal devices which a rising amount of people are buying for personal use in order to improve their nighttime. K2 meters Ouija Boards, Dowsing Rods and other products to aid in ghost hunting are purchased from a variety of websites.

It is important to remember that the more time you spend in events like an event like a hunt or a ghost hunt weekend the greater enjoyment you are likely to get from the experience. While they've got plenty of experience to impart, the team responsible for the event can just do a little in order to move people You may find your voice to be most effective in getting spirits to talk the most. Get involved and speak up when you feel especially brave, inquire whether you could hold an vigil even if you're not with anyone else.

Remember that regardless of where your ghostly adventures will take you, make the most of every chance and relish every second of it. It could be the most thrilling experience you've ever had with your lights turned off.

Ghost Studies - How to Learn About Ghost Hunting From Home

Many people are fascinated by the paranormal but aren't sure what to do. In response the short-term courses in the paranormal have started being offered by some public and community colleges. The goal of these courses is to teach interested people on various topics related to paranormal activity.

If you say to people you're going to university to research ghosts, you may be seen as bizarre. There are just as many skeptical people as well as believers in paranormal investigation like there are people who believe. The course in ghost research may be the perfect course is needed if you're a enthusiast of supernatural phenomena. The aim of this class is to instruct you on how to study haunted and paranormal locations instruments and equipment, strategies used, and foremost taking precautions and safety measures to be aware of.

These are some of the most important characteristics of the fundamental courses in ghost research:

1. It should be written keeping your interests with your level of interest in mind. It shouldn't be overly technical or complicated for those who are just beginning.

2. The church must not be intolerance of any religion. It must be as neutral as it can be the part that is religious.

3. The course must be developed to be organized in a way that is easy to comprehend. Courses must be broken into sections that are appropriate for students as they're typically very short.

4. It should address the primary issues that beginners have. The majority of people

just beginning their journey are curious about the best way to begin. In contrast advanced investigators of paranormal investigations study the complexities of hunting and have developed sophisticated techniques to track and locate haunted places.

5. Teachers who have a thorough understanding of the paranormal must be able to instruct the class. They should have a theoretical understanding of investigations into paranormal phenomena as well as a knowledge of the field of research and investigation.

6. You must have a money-back warranty if you read about ghosts online from a source.

7. The most recent techniques for ghost hunting and applications of the latest high-end equipment and tools must be taught in the course. Computer applications must

be included that include the use of programs for data management and storage.

What is the best way to Study Ghost Hunting Online In the end, investigating paranormal phenomena is a lucrative job or an enjoyable activity. Find a reliable school that you are able to learn about ghost hunting in a safe and secure manner is vital.

The new TV shows Ghost Hunters, Ghost Hunters International, Most Haunted, and Paranormal State have been a major factor in the rise of curiosity in ghost hunts. Each of the shows is to find proof to support or deny the notion of a genuine ghost when you enter a home or a building in which paranormal events are reported or felt. It's extremely challenging to prove that a ghost is real.

Television viewers are unable to truly experience ghost hunters' experience. The ghost hunters feel many private emotions like the fear of anxiety, stress as well as coldness. They also have feeling that the emotions they feel cannot be perceived by anyone else. It is impossible to know everything you can about ghost hunting until you've been to one for your own. While you won't require any specific equipment for on a ghost hunt, it's beneficial to carry some.

The video camera is essential to monitor and capture all things that happen. It's best to own multiple cameras. A friend and you can have a camera each and take pictures of each other as well as any events that occur around you when you are traveling together.

Digital camera: You should capture a large amount of still images when you believe there's something around you even though you aren't able to see it. Things you cannot see are often captured by cameras.

Pen and paper: Be certain to record all that you notice and also when the event occurred. Hunts like this can go on until the very early hours of early morning. This makes it hard to keep track of specific times or events, if you do not note them down.

The distinction between spirits and ghosts.

It is evident when you attend a haunted gathering because there's lots of conversation about communication with spirits. However, the term "spirit" appears to be utilized whenever there's some activity, ghosts are also talked about. They are vastly different. A ghost occurs an entity that is apparent to other people but unaware of it. It isn't affected by any devices or attempts to contact it. the ghost will act as normal. It's essentially inactive and has no idea of who we are. Imagine repeating the same routine for a prolonged duration of time, such like walking to the newspaper shop each morning around 7 a.m. following the same path for the last 30 years, it would be an appropriate method to explain the phenomenon. The behaviour's energy is trapped. It's like watching a video clip repeatedly with no emotion attached. Many people who experience the ghosts who wander around are experiencing ghosts of someone else.

Spirits are, however are an entirely distinct creature. Spirits are able to interact with us, and also have an effect on us. It can physically contact us and change our environment. It is not just visible, energy can be visible. Changes in temperature as well as knocking and tapping and even poltergeist activities. They are all signs which spirit could do. In the event that we learn that spirits can't harm us, and later witness the flinging of stones, and the people who are allegedly getting taken over by spirit that is quite perplexing. When we encounter ghosts, it is almost like we are merely spectators of our past lives which is presented before us. You need to be more alert and aware in the event of spirit manifestation. People who have had contact with spirits know that it can very alarming and disturbing especially when it is communicating to us. There are thousands of books that deal with spirits and ghosts; in this post, I wanted to remind readers that there's a huge different between these two entities and assist them in understanding the underlying issues when discussing them as part of an investigation into ghosts.

Chapter 7: What Are Ghosts And Why Do We Hunt Them?

If you asked more than a dozen paranormal experts the question, you'd most likely receive a variety of solutions. The subject of ghosts is a good opportunity to let your mind wander an ounce and allow your imagination to roam. The first step is to look into the standard definition of ghosts before proceeding to my own view.

GHOST - NOUN - DEFINITION

The apparition of a dead individual thought to manifest or apparent to living people in the form of a vague representation.

Here's the information in plain English. Ghosts are merely an image of a previously living creature. Simple, right? It's possible to make the bow, but it can do little to explain to our readers what the concept of a spirit is. Put down our dictionary. Here's my take on the subject that has been honed by countless ghost hunts.

Your Shell, Your Spirit.

Have a look at your reflection. Are you able to look at your body, or the flesh? All that is part of the physical form of your body is an outer shell. The essence of you is the spark that is beneath. You are the person inside your head. It is the constant dialogue that doesn't stop. Your ego is brain, soul and intellect that are all rolled into one being. If you die or that your body stops functioning the collection of thoughts that will continue to be a part of you.

In the field of physics, there's a conservation law which says that energy cannot be destroyed or createdIt simply shifts from one container to another.

There's a great deal of technical jargon into this notion, however, you do not need to understand it all this moment. The soul of our being, or whatever it is it is, is made up of energy. As soon as our body is gone then our soul is liberated and the energy that we carry on.

If I am in an old medical facility and use my EVP monitor, I'm in contact with someone who is represented through their energy. It is this individual who once lived in the fleshy shell, but this time they have been stripped of physical appearance. You're not wrong for the fact that you're already turning off me. It's a difficult concept to take in and is more difficult to weigh against the many religions of the world. The faith in ghosts is a violation of the majority of religions, but that's another subject to come up with.

Dealing in Demons.

Perhaps you're in agreement in my view of energy from the spirit world, however it may leave you thinking about the existence of demons and poltergeists. If you've even spent one minute exploring the paranormal, you've probably heard about these troublemakers from the spiritual realm. What is the best way to weigh the idea of individual spirituality against things that could never ever been truly human?

The notion of demonic beings can be traced as far back as Greek mythology even though the significance of the term has evolved in the course of the years. Demons, as we have come to know their names, have become popular thanks to Christian faith as well as Hollywood made entertainment. However, the origin of demons cannot be found here, nor is it there. Here we are to talk about what demons actually are.

The most common definition of demons is the devil is a evil spirit who will do harm to you.

This is another dictionary definition, which connects the words with an elegant bow. But, there's much more to this that we cannot explain using simple terms.

Based on my own experience, which is thankfully modest in this area Demons are spirits that symbolize our basic and negative needs. They're spirits who seek to cause harm in every manner they are able to. It could be manifested in creating a sense of discord between family members, encouraging violence and even physical possession. Films often go wrong when it comes to supernatural phenomena, however possession can be just as real and terrifying.

The Bible is a good source. Bible to see what we think is a precise description of what demon can be:

MATTHEW 12:43, KING JAMES VERSION

If the spirit of uncleanness is extinguished from a human He walks through deserted spots, searching for rest and finds none.

If you take the Bible seriously in this respect you'd have concluded that demons existed at one time humans. In this chapter, we conclude that demons are human spirits who were evicted away from their bodies because of their own bad deeds. Their goal for these demon creatures is currently to discover a new place to reside in. or, at most, to unleash their frustration on living to cause another's life just the same as it once was. Demons are envious of those who live. They seek to eat away your energy. They would like to live in your body. They'd like to cause harm. If this isn't enough to scare you, and you're not ready to go on.

Hunting Ghosts: A Noble Pursuit.

If you're adamant about my statements, you have a clear understanding of what spirits are, or better than that, what they might be. Are you able to accept the words? Are you still tempted to connect with dead people? We were thinking we did. Let's discuss the reasons the reasons why you shouldn't and should go on a ghost hunt.

Many people search for the realm of spirit for the purpose of finding the lost person they loved. They would like to be in contact with the spirit they had in their the physical form. We don't recommend ghost hunting, if that's your reason for coming to us. If you go after ghosts, you're opening yourself to their presence. A person who is emotional raw and seeking closure, exposes their soul to demons and they risk their lives. For all matters that could be dangerous, we advise to be careful. Don't be a slave to this idea and look for some other avenues to find closure.

I would suggest exploring the realm of ghost hunting with the most noble motive knowledge. There's no endeavor more noble than knowing, and I believe that we are obligated to learn as much as we can about the universe that surrounds us. If you are able to embrace the notions of spirit, and pursuing their ideas with the tools that you're about to master that you will complete your knowledge of what living truly is. Is there a reason that is more important?

Chapter 8: What Tools Will I Need?

If you've got this far, I can tell you're determined to find alternative options. That is why I'm about allow you to pore through my tried and tested combat-tested ghost hunting methods. Just like everything else, it is necessary to be prepared for ghost hunting to be successful. It means that you'll have to master methods, acquire equipment and refine your mentality. We'll start by learning the fundamentals.

Ghost Hunting Toolbox.

One of my top television series that is paranormal is Ghost Adventures. Though you could have views on the credibility of the series but you cannot deny how prepared the team is before starting every investigation. The reason this team is innovative is the fact that they are continually pushing the limits with regard to technological advancements in ghost hunting. They have always a latest device in their arsenal. The majority of them have a bad reputation, however a handful that work are good. Our belief is that any study should begin by making a properly-constructed toolbox. We'll take a peek at my own toolbox.

1. Digital Audio Recorder

The very first item that you must incorporate into your toolbox is inexpensive and easy to find one: a digital audio recorder. There's no device that is more essential or complex than this one. In a way that isn't fully comprehend, ghosts are known to speak via these devices by way of EVPs. A EVP is simply an acronym for electronic voice phenomenon. When you are in an EVP session, you'll ask questions to the spooky room. If you replay the recording, if you have the chance, you may get a response from a person who is. It is possible to find a recording device on Amazon with a price of less than thirty dollars. You should bring a couple of these devices along with you on your next trip for a look.

Personal Experience: The digital recorder I have is my top piece of equipment I have. When I was filming a segment on Project Paranormal one of my photographers put up an audio recorder before preparing their cameras. In the recording device, I heard my cameraman say "Sorry for all of the noise" while looking through her bag. After that, it was clear as the day, a female voice was followed by the words, "Be quiet!" The woman was the sole female inside the building.

2. Digital Camcorder

The largest acquisition you'll be required to buy when starting the journey of ghost hunting will be the camera. It is recommended to purchase a camera which can capture in Infrared Ultraviolet, Infrared, and Full Spectrum. Recording while lighting is off is essential. The reasons for this in the future, but for now you can rely on us for this. Go to Amazon or the local electronics shop to find options which fit within your budget. I've had excellent success with in the Bell & Howell line of IR cameras and cost less than $200.

Personal Experience: I was looking into the third level, which was an attic of a house in preparation for the next episode of Project Paranormal. We had multiple cameras set up simultaneously in one of our EVP sessions. The "B" Cam captured an object flying in the air before landing on the A Cam. The battery of the 'A' Cam failed to last for a while despite being completely recharged.

3. EMF Detector

We believe that ghosts are an energy representation of our soul. This is why the use of an EMF detector will help in being able to detect spirits. EMF detectors can cost a lot in the case of top brands, however their price increase is well worth the cost. Imagine yourself cruising through your life searching for something which isn't perceived. Then, think about the fact that EMF Detectors are an electronic device that allows the user to pinpoint what they want to find. They are a valuable tool. A EMF detector should not be the sole tool for investigating but it is a good accessory tool. Make sure you are aware of any false EMF readings.

My personal experience - I am working across the Schiller Piano Factory in Oregon, IL during an overnight study. The factory was not the energy that was sensitive enough to be detected by our device. It had been several hours and not spotted any trace of energy on the EMF detector. Then, while we were walking along, our EMF detector started to begin to beep. Then we immediately settled down for the EVP session. We were able to record voice recordings right there and then following a long period of the night in silence.

4. Spirit Box Research Device

Ghost Adventures singlehandedly inspired an whole generation of researchers studying paranormal phenomena with the introduction of their Spirit Box Research device. I have the SB7 version, that is a model older which I've found invaluable in investigation. The Spirit Box is essentially a broken radio which quickly scans FM or AM frequencies on an radio. When it's operating at the right speed, it will only emit pure white background noise. Why is this beneficial? I believe that the Spirit Box opens up a channel for spirits to connect.

Once you have turned on the Spirit Box it is recommended to begin asking questions. If you sense spirits in the room around you, you'll hear a voice resound over the sounds. If it is a wise spirit, it will be able to answer inquiries.

My personal experience Personal Experience: I was working on an investigation in the famed Ashmore Estates in Ashmore, IL. My friend and I were in the area that was once an exclusive kitchen that was used by both children and women. We were sweeping the floor the floor with one of our Spirit Box for about five or six minutes, while we asked questions. The Spirit Box had not spoken. Then I thought of asking the people in the room "Are you afraid that two men are in your kitchen?" In a half second afterwards, it was the Spirit Box spoke for the first time and said "No". The voice was bright as a star and I'm still experiencing the chills just thinking about the experience. The room became a blaze of energy and spirituality for us.

5. Audio Editing Software

If you intend to become involved in this area, you will require the necessary tools in order you can properly evaluate your findings. We recommend downloading the software for free Audacity to improve the audio files you have. Audacity is a basic application that allows you to tidy up your audio files, and also increase the prominence of the voices you record.

Personal Experience: While certain spirits appear to speak directly to our recorders but others do not even register. With Audacity I'm able to eliminate as much sound as I can while increasing the frequency of what the spirit of our soul is hearing.

They are the instruments that I always carry on my body always. It is also recommended to grab an excellent flashlight, extra batteries for the devices you use, and also an air mask in case you're planning to investigate the ruins of structures. Any evidence of paranormal activity is not worthy of causing harm to your breathing system.

Chapter 9: My Favorite Ghost Hunting Techniques

The process of hunting for ghosts is kind as a painting art. The trick is being aware of the broad strokes in the art, however should you master all the small details, you will be able to do a better job. In this article, we will discuss some of the different ghost-hunting strategies you can use on your next search. I've tried all these techniques to various levels of satisfaction. What you'll discover is that trying something new is more effective than doing nothing. There is no way to know what might cause a reaction to your Other Side. So, without further delay...

The Essentials.

1. The Burst Session Recording EVPs can be equally exciting and awe-inspiring. Most of the time, you don't realize that you've recorded anything until you arrive home and examine the audio recordings.

Burst Sessions can be a great way to capture a moment immediately. To get a burst Session to be successful, you need to discover a spot that appears to radiate something of a certain energy. Be aware of your body as well as your EMF detectors. Spirits may manifest by draining your energy and leading you to feel tired or dizzy -- and even freezing. If you experience one of these signs, immediately begin recording your digital device. You should record around 60 seconds of questions. Make sure you pause for a sufficient amount of time between each question. Play back the video that you recorded. Wear headphones for a close-up listen. There is a chance that you will capture an EVP that can lead your inquiry into a completely new direction.

2. Individual Sessions: Imagine you're a spirit. It's hard to be at peace within the

space is your home. A few minutes later, six or five people arrive in your space with guns aplenty with recording equipment, cameras as well as Spirit Boxes and other things. It's possible to want to stay hidden from them, but why not? Sessions with a solo person can be great methods to bring out timid thoughts. Invite an investigator or simply go in a space completely by yourself. You can conduct the EVP as well as a Spirit Box session without any others in the room. Sometime the most captivating and chilling proof is captured in this manner.

3. Triggers and Objects: The most crucial technique you should be aware of is bringing some props to your investigation. If I was conducting the investigation at an older VFW For instance you could bring pieces of the soldier's uniform. In reality, any item related to the spirit's possible era might be of use. It is your goal to provoke

an emotional response in the spirit and prompt the spirit to show up and display themselves by some means.

4. Your Body - Ultimately, you'll need to utilize your body as a tool to conduct your research. It will be easy to recognize that you are in the presence of spirit much faster than the devices. In rooms, I've experienced the temperature dropping. My arms are tingling and I've felt goosebumps. While it's happening, I'm recording voices on my computer that I could have realized had I not been attentive. One of my best incidents occurred in an old kitchen in the Ashmore Estates. I was doing an Spirit Box session when my companion, Christopher, kept seeing orbs appear on the screen of his IR monitor. While the orbs started manifesting, I was beginning feeling weak and dizzy. Therefore, I stopped in the Spirit Box and went over to the man. While we

were discussing and I was distracted when a voice began saying something in the audio recorder that we left in the space. "I'm Sorry" it said to us. It's impossible to know what the meaning of the spirit was, however I'm still shivering just thinking about the incident.

Other Techniques.

1. Provocation - It's probably going be the most controversial choice on our list however we think it's a good idea to be included. Provocation demands that you bring an angry and passionate approach in the EVP sessions. This is essentially asking your inner self to take action and hoping that the aggression will yield results. Be careful when you use this method since you might not like the results you get.

2. Photographing at night if you own cameras that are equipped by an IR light or an option for flash, then it is possible to

try this approach. Your photographer should lead in the corridors of your house. The photographer will snap flash photos directly in front of you trying to catch something that is manifesting itself in the night. There are some wild and interesting evidence that could be captured in this manner.

3. Thermometers - This method can be utilized together with the other choices in our selection. In general, it's believed that the spirits of manifestation leave cold spots within their path. The use of a thermometer digital with a laser measurement device will aid in finding particular cold areas and track these spots to monitor. There have been times when temperatures are about 70° before falling in the wake of an entity manifesting. I've stood there in shock and watched my thermometer go down up to 10 degrees.

It's a terrifying experience but it's documented.

4. Rituals - There's an aspect of me that is intrigued by the idea of using old-fashioned rituals. As I've mentioned repeatedly -There are certain doors that should not be closed. Even though using rituals drawn from texts of the past or for that matter, using the internet might seem appealing, they aren't worthwhile. While we're all experienced, as it might be, we're just not as experienced. Let the church handle rituals and adhere to the fundamental strategies we've discussed previously. It will be better for you. doing this.

Chapter 10: Putting Together Your Ghost Hunting Team

The whole exploring the paranormal by yourself. It is not necessary to be a part of a team to gather amazing evidence. In that regard, it would be remiss of us to not suggest you put together a group. Joining forces with people who share the same fascination with the paranormal could enrich your research as well as provide an opportunity for having a bonding experience over. However, it is important to be cautious about the people you decide to join with. It is time to establish your own personal ghost hunting group.

1. Look Local.

If you are looking to put together the ghost hunting group, you'll need to find people who live in your region. Though this could sound like a daunting task for you, particularly if you are in the middle of the Midwest do not be concerned. Ghost hunters are all over the place and all you need is a handful of appropriate questions to locate them. You can visit sites such as Facebook or Craigslist for a search for groups of ghost hunters in your area. You'll likely find one local to your location already. If they aren't, think about the creation of a webpage and people will come across your page. Or, you could look into the deepest parts of Internet. There are numerous networks for ghost hunters on the Internet and our favorite resource is PARANORMALSOCIETIES.COM. The site can serve as an excellent source of information.

2. Learn to be comfortable and say"no.

The realm of ghost hunting is a place where you can find people of every kind. It is possible to find those who are a bit loose. There are also the most compassionate and intelligent individuals around. While you are for a hunt with ghosts, you're exposing yourself to the ghosts in the space and to the other people in the vicinity. It is essential to feel at ease with individuals around you to be successful. If you're not a good fit with someone, then no one is obliged to go on looking for you.

3. Beware of the tension.

Ghost hunters can appear as if they're characters on some SyFy Network television show. They'll always be telling the same story and some experience and will always appear to be able to outwit your investigation. Even though we're not keen to label people as liars particularly in this area however, it is important to be cautious about who you research. If you are in a field that requires integrity and honesty, linking your self to an impulsive or a person with a soaring personality could waste your time of your time. It's easy to discern the distinction between thrill seekers and genuine ghost hunter.

4. Set your limits.

If you are going on a ghost hunt, it is important to establish the boundaries you want to set and be aware of your boundaries. If you're going on a ghost hunt with your companion, you'll need ensure that you know what your boundaries are. If you don't feel comfortable by yourself in a dark and filthy basement, your friend must be aware of. Additionally, certain people tend to be drawn by evil spirits using unorthodox strategies (Ouija Boards, Provocation and Demon Luring) and we recommend avoid these methods. The real world isn't like the films or the movies, so real-life ghost hunting isn't something you should be frightened of.

5. Identify strengths/weaknesses.

Everyone is unique so we all have strengths and flaws. Think about creating your team of ghost hunters like you would make a football or a basketball squad. It was apparent early on that I excelled at keeping cool, calm and focussed. But, I'm an emotional closed-off person. A friend of mine was fascinated by ghost hunting. He was extremely open emotionally. He had a great sense of empathy and I was able to tell right away that he'd make a wonderful ally for EVP sessions. Thus, I invited him to join us as a guide during our search. He managed to bring amazing photos which I'm not sure that I'd be able to get.

6. Enjoy yourself.

Then you need to ensure that your group of ghost hunters are enjoying the experience. If you're not getting paid, the focus should be in creating an enjoyable experience and profitable for all those involved. Ghost hunting is a exciting adventure, but it must be a positive experience is always sought for. If you have a coworker who is rude, overbearing or rude, then it is likely that you will have negative outcomes. Although your primary focus should be on proof prior to anything else, your primary goal should be on creating pleasant experiences.

Chapter 11: Conducting Your First Ghost Hunt

The largest step of an investigator's life is completing their first investigation. It's likely that you've been in your home in front of your EVP audio recorders. Perhaps you've even participated in on a different investigation an entirely different team. In this article, however, we will discuss making an investigation of our own. Let me tell you a of my initial investigation, and then begin to lay out the fundamentals for the initial investigation.

Don't Make My Mistakes.

After recording my first EVP after recording my first ever EVP, I determined to plunge myself into the abyss of investigating ghosts. I felt an unstoppable urge to gather all the tools I could locate, with a handful of willing acquaintances and possibly a haunted place that I could visit. I wasn't thinking about things in a comprehensive manner and in the end, I injured myself during the course of my adventure.

My initial full-blown study was at The Schiller Piano Factory which is situated within Oregon, IL. The structure was constructed around 1890 and was operating as a piano for many years. My reason for choosing the location I did was because I am from the area and I was familiar with the proprietor I was confident that I was able to get into the building easily. Is it often you're going to come across a hookup like that? It was an enormous three-story structure with an interesting history I was able to walk through completely free. What did I do wrong?

For starters, I was definitely approaching this building from the wrong direction. It was like I was already familiar with the location and also the structure therefore I did not need to conduct any investigation. It's one of the most common sins in ghost hunting: be aware of the exact location of your haunted house. Understanding the past of the place can lead you in asking the correct type of questions to trigger the spirit of. With regard to Schiller, the only thing I knew was that it was used to have been a piano factory. I didn't know there was an utterly devastating fire that erupted on the 1st floor nearly fifty years back. Shouldn't I have walked through the building in the event that I knew? However, I didn't. It wasn't the only error that I'd made.

For the sake of my research to finish, I found myself limiting my own evidence that I could record. It was clear that I wanted the aid of a digital audio recorder so that I could record EVP actions, but I did not have any idea when or how often to use the machine. The thing I was able to do was to only run my digital recorder while in a position to have the EVP session. Why is this happening? It's true that I was in the factory for about eight hours, and only came in a little over 30 minutes worth of recorded audio using my recorder digital. The math is easy. Today, I carry several audio recorders, and I keep one in use. When I am investigating, I use my always-on monitor in order to take notes. When I spot a unexpected activity on my EMF detector, then I don't need to bother using my recording equipment and I'll be able to jump directly into the issue.

In the end, I was not prepared for the things I'd discover and the significance of being able to take something to take home. I walked into the Lion's Den with a tender steak in my palms. Was I prepared for what was going to transpire? In the moment, I had no knowledge of spirits or demons. I had my eyes closed in spirituality I was completely unaware of the things I might discover. After I have learned the risks and dangers that come with ghost hunting, I am better prepared myself.

That's my biggest mistakes I'd to make when I began investigating ghosts. Are you prepared to plan your first hunt? Let's get deep into the investigation and go through each step you'll have to take so that you can conduct an extremely solid investigation.

Your First Hunt.

1. Find your location.

If you've seen shows such as Paranormal Lockdown or Ghost Adventures and you're likely to believe that the only method to connect with spirit being visiting these elaborately haunted places. There is no doubt that some structures can serve as hubs of religious activity, but it isn't a reason to consider the smaller things. Consider locating an older structure in your area. Study the background of it. If something catches your attention, and you want to add the place on your list of possible locations. There doesn't have to be dead bodies in a structure for it to be spiritually active. It's been around for a long time and has seen people move across the globe, leaving impressions of energy.

2. Assess your requirements.

Let's suppose that you're looking into a ruined three-story house that has a limestone basement. What do you have to do? For starters, you'll want to determine the season of the year during which you will be conducting your hunt. Are you in a cold climate? Is the place heated? Wear gloves, jackets, and hats to remain warm. Allow your spirits bring you chills. The next step is sketching out your building inside your head. What number of people will you be conducting an investigation? How many cameras do you need? Do you have any additional audio recorders to accommodate everyone? Being fully prepared for your team before the commencement of the research is the most effective thing that you could do to your search. It is possible to take your team out to various locations for individual investigation is a wonderful feeling.

3. Select your method.

The most thrilling part of any investigation into ghosts is in the dark and your strategy is executed. In my research into my investigation into the Ashmore Estates I wanted to be sure to give myself an opportunity to seek for specific spirits. It was believed that the Ashmore Estates had been a place for those suffering from mental illness and physically incapacitated. There was a lovely young lady who resided in the residence and lost her life to fire. It was reported of her presence within the structure and my intention during the evening was to talk with her to bring the peace and joy she needed. Thus, I took an item that she could have fun with. When I went to find the child, I took care regarding my voice as well as the words I chose to use as well as my overall manner of speaking. I wanted to appear friendly rather than intimidating. My goal when entering Ashmore was to provide an energizing presence for the young child. Look around at the structure which you are planning to explore determine your plan of action.

4. Make sure you hit your targets.

The most frustrating scenario when you finish an investigation, only realizing that you haven't captured enough video or audio for analysis in the future. Prior to beginning your investigation, prepare a checklist of the areas that you'd like to study and the various techniques you'd like to use. Refer to my book on Ghost Hunting Techniques' and use the techniques when suitable. Make sure that you have multiple people test every method to determine the results you achieve. The more data you accumulate, the greater likely you'll be able to capture some interesting information.

5. Be patient during your hunt.

Today, we live in an age that is characterized by instant gratification, which can cause us to be bored or even disinterested rapidly. If you are interested in investigating ghosts, you must know that the majority of your time is being secluded, at night. Naturally, you'll be having fun but it's not an action-packed, fast-paced adventure that TV shows will make you believe. There are literally a handful of hours cut out from each episode. The highlights of an hour or more investigation. Don't lose hope. Accept it as a part of the journey and accept it.

6. Review your results.

Your investigation is just the first step in your job. After you have completed your investigation, you will have many hours of video footage and hours of audio recordings as well as a few files full of photos. Although this may seem like a daunting and daunting job, it's not your responsibility to go through every single one of your files in search of any evidence of ghost activity. Get a good pair of headphones, and then upload the files to your laptop. You can relax and listen to every single file, while writing off on your timesheet for any possible discoveries. It will be surprising what you discover. Do not feel pressured to go through all of it at one time. It is possible to delegate portions of your documents to others on your team.

Chapter 12: Torches Lighting

The very first aspect we'd want to discuss is lighting. It is a very crucial things you'll require in your investigation due to many reasons.

To investigate the reports of ghosts or spirits its essential be capable of seeing your surroundings and in some way.

The best light tool is the 3 in 1 Lantern made by RAC. Price PS20 PS40

For a paranormal society it's a great idea to keep a spot light or torch, as well as a lantern.

Spotlights work well in huge areas and also outdoors for seeing distant distances. For the indoor explorations that can be closed off, while the lantern is perfect for an areas where you have to get a wider perspective of things like caves, tunnels and so on.

UV Torch

UV is the abbreviation for ultraviolet that is a distinct light spectrum that is used for ghost hunts. Price PS5 PS25

There are many reasons individuals use this method. among them is for the eye to be trained to be able to perceive NEAR UV which is why certain people believe it is.

ghosts may be lurking in various wavelengths of light that are difficult to detect such as UV and IR which is the abbreviation for infrared.

Another option is to pair it with your Camcorder or digital flash camera that has the capability to detect the UV as well as IR spectrum.

IR Torch Illuminator

Infrared is a term used to describe infrared. It's very common in paranormal research mostly to aid the night vision camera see an additional field. I would not recommend using a small IR torch since it's not going to make any an impact on the camera's capacity to detect IR. I'd recommend an IR illumination device that fits the same style as a CCT camera. PS5 PS80. Based the IR distance.

If you buy an adaptor for 9V cctv clips it is possible to connect this adaptor to the above cctv illumination device and then run it off a 9v battery. Instead of having to find a power socket The next item you'd have to purchase is an accessory for flashing one.

Hot shoe that connects this light source to the camcorder

If you own Sony camcorders, you may find an intelligent hotshoe built that allows you to use with IR illuminations from Sony. Price PS40 PS70.

Wildlife Camera's

They are mostly used for taking images of wildlife or exotic animals, they come in many different designs, and dimensions. They are usually small and easy to transport, and

Make use of an SDHC card, which allows you to directly transfer images to your laptop

With the help of on the card, they are able to shoot video or images using motion settings as well as regular.

How can you use this to help with ghost hunting?

It is a good idea to make this an object to trigger, for example the camera that is in the photo is equipped with two sensors. after the sensors have detected any movement, the camera can take photos using IR light sources over the sensors.

It is possible to alter the sensitivity of sensors, and you can add time stamps, moon phase

Price around PS90 180.

I'd recommend utilizing the camera to capture wildlife in places where you're unlikely to be to, then look over any images you've taken in the course of examination.

Strobe Light

If you're unfamiliar with the paranormal world, you might be wondering how come strobe lights are used?

Every day, there are individuals like us seeking out innovative and new methods for exploring the paranormal. And this one is among these. In the nightclub with many strobes flashing.. What are you likely to observe? Frames of people move around because the strobe can slow your eyesight every time it flashes. The idea could be that! ghosts can move that rapidly that our eyes are unable to be able to see them. So this strobe can to slow our eyes and possibly even spot something that is supernatural?

The majority of strobes are white Light however in the world of the paranormal it might be a great option to buy a diverse ranges of light, ultraviolet and IR. You could purchase infrared LEDs placed onto the glass of the strobos to block out all visible white light. It also allows in ultraviolet and infrared. Price PS10 PS40.

It is important to note that this can cause harm to other people affected by epilepsy. Therefore, it is recommended to consult all members of your team before using these devices as part of your investigation.

IR Thermometers

Again, it is a very wellknown device in paranormal investigations

The device monitors temperatures of the environment while conducting an investigation. Very simple to operate. It has an LCD screen that gives you the temperature The majority of thermometers come with an IR light that takes measurements of the object that the it hits at a specific distance. This makes it ideal for taking the temperature of people during investigations. If you want to measure temperatures in a space, it's ideal to turn off the IR beam to ensure that there isn't an individual temperature for a particular item. There are thermometers available for purchase for sale from PS10 to PS80.

Chapter 13: Evp Equipment

EVP is an acronym for Electronic voice phenomenon It is the most used term for ghost searching. A EVP can be described as when you make recordings on a particular device, and during the replay there is something you don't know was present when you made the recording.

If you are able to hear something whilst making recordings, this will not constitute an EVP it would instead be a voicerelated phenomenon, so it is important not to label any Voice manifestation as an EVP when writing your reports and so on.

The best way to conduct EVPS is to begin your session by stating the time and Date as well as the location. In the beginning, mention who's present and note any interaction that you are currently hearing. Make sure that there are only two individuals speaking in the meeting, where they alternate to ask questions.

Allowing 10 to 15 seconds between turns in order to respond. Also, it is important to label any sound heard that isn't within the audio recording in order to avoid the possibility of false evps in looking over.

The next step is to examine a few EVP equipment.

EVP Recorder (Dictaphone)

There are many options to buy Dictaphones at a variety of locations and range between PS15 to PS80

Based on the model and model, the one that is most popular is Olympus according to my experience. This model above is the model vn2100PC.

It's a good idea to locate a device that supports PC USB. Fast backups of data such as the one mentioned below.

The most frequent issue with Dictaphones are that moving about may cause wind sound effects on recordings which is why it's recommended that you put on the floor your recorder in order to avoid this.

Additional Note Don't set the phone next to EMF meters because there are magnets within their records that EMF meters can detect.

Zoom h2

It is a professional recording device that captures stereo sound featuring a total of 4 microphones that are capable of recording your surroundings in 360 degrees, which records authentic stereo sound, and lets you switch between

by using different microphone pickups that can activate the microphone. It is used for radio and podcast work as well as music recording.

Standard Dictaphones recorder, 80 Degrees or less, that is equipped with

There is less likelihood of recording the authentic sound of the environment. It has a lot of advantages that are too numerous to mention. The device is also connected to the tripod

One of the advantages of these recorders for professionals is they support live audio that could be used to create realtime evp recording. You can hear EVPS in real time without having to play back the recorder. If you hear LIVE EVPs it's best to record the exact time that you listened to the EVP so that you can easily review it before you copy the evp file. Note down the information is prior to

If you want to classify it as being an EVP it is essential to confirm that nobody else has had heard the sound other than the person who heard it. A way to circumvent that would be to label the sound as

They happen in the course of investigation therefore if they mentioned a vehicle was passing or you hear a vehicle passing, you'll know this isn't an EVP.

Price PS90 PS130

More technological

If you're looking to take the limits of EVP, it is possible to purchase the wireless sound transmitter, or an enormous cable jack. You can then connect the zoom h2 straight into your laptop using the software Audacity and Digital Wave Pad.

This will let you observe the distinct spikes in the EVP recording as well as capture the realtime ambiance in the space. It is best to have a person to watch the EVP passing through the line creating logs, so it's much easier to take from this EVP.

EFP

Chapter 14: The Efp Stands For Evp Field Processor

It is a black box, with a vubar graph. It plugs in to an LIVE audio EVP recorder. You can then connect your earphones into the headphone socket on the EFP.

The gadget amplifies the sound of what you are recording by transmitting the audio to your headphones The best way to do this is to get the Jack cable, then plug it into the headphone socket. This will lead to another recording device. This way, you can record the atmosphere that the device enhances.

It is possible to set the White noise tones using the dial located on the left side of the screen, that will move the VU chart both up and down it is best to achieve is to level it up to the RED middle, and then it is possible to monitor any spikes or spikes that occur on the VU chart.

And as Price PS50 100

EMF Meters

EMF refers to Electromagnetic field. The phrase is frequently used in paranormal research.

There is a belief that spirits, ghosts and other entities are made up of EMF fields. As such, individuals utilize EMF meters to establish their validity; however there are numerous things that may affect these meters including cellphones, wifi, Electronics in general. It's generally quite simple to identify the causes that affect the meters; at least one out of 10 places there will be an odd EMF measurement that we can't identify with anything that is happening in the area.

K2 Meter

The most popular ghost searching EMF gauge is the k2 Meter with five lights on the uppermost part of the device that will show the field strength. There are four versions of this device, and with each new model comes with the possibility of a tiny perk. Its price range is PS35 between PS35 and PS80 Based on the model.

Version 1 A typical meters with pushin or off that must be pressing in order for it to perform. It's an issue due to the fact that it's so difficult to loose your grip and get incorrect results.

Version 2 The same as above, however you do not have to press the button to keep it pressed

Version Three

Similar to the above, but equipped with a red LED to the other side of the meter.

Version Four (Rare)

Similar to Version 2 that has an input jack integrated in the bottom of the unit. The idea allows you to connect an audio speaker or a voice recorder through a jack or just put in headphones to hear the EMF field as they occur. K2 Meter Other information These meters behave exactly the same when they have low batteries is present, and the initial light will appear a bit dim and the second LED will flash at times. The Full readings will appear every occasionally, and until the battery has been replaced It is recommended to use replacing the battery at every examination to prevent false results. The Version 4 info sheet tells users to utilize a microphone or a recorder to plug directly into the device. The latter could give inaccurate results also because both devices contain magnets that could affect the k2 gauge in the event of moving them.

ELF Zone Meter

The Elf zone meter is a basic meter, with three lighting fixtures built into the base. A sturdy construction, quick motion can be a problem for most meters. However, in this one it's not. The sensitivity of the meter isn't very high. It is a good choice that you use it if you're just beginning to set with it since it's around

PS10 PS15.00.

Green (safe) Orange (caution) Red (Danger)

Gauss Master

Another wellknown meter out in the field. Equipped with a scale that will give you a reading including normal and high.

Sensitivity setting. If a reading is high, it'll sound like a buzzer. This is a very sensitive meter. The typical price is PS20 between PS20 and PS30.

Another issue with this type of meter is that the buzzer will continue to go off even though the reading is actually gone. Also, speedy movements can impact the measurement. Therefore, it is important to walk at a slow pace..

Electrosmog (Esmog)

It is, in my opinion, a more affordable variant of the K2 Meter that is more robust. It is a square unit that has an on and off switch on the side along with a bar graph of lights along the scale of numbers. Two versions are available.

This device is similar to the one above, with the only distinction is a buzzer. Its price is PS20 or PS25 that is affordable and worthy of the money for any user.

EMF Tester

The device is square equipped with a circular probe to it. It acts as a sensor for EMF fields. It has 3 settings available on the device. It also has an LCD display which displays what the reading of the Field is. The device is ideal for reading scientific data for your staff. We have not found any issues using this gadget and typically cost between PS45 or PS60

Trifield meter

It's a costly device with four options, including an Needle gauge graph that is highly sensitive. The gauge is so sensitive that it detects the earth's magnetism.

The settings include as follows Battery Test Electric Magnetic Ion Sum. Each field is utilized to fulfill a number of different purposes. to discover natural field that may actually cause an activity, Ion Sum is both magnetic and electric fields that it is able to detect.

Additional notes One theory available is ghosts consist of Electrostatic or microwaves. If you moved magnetic field, it could transform to an Electrostatic field, instead of magnetic. In theory, if you were to see you were to see a ghost, it would be an Electrostatic field.

It is real and "not moving" it would have the magnetic field.

Cell Censor

Another meter that is like the Gauss Master This is a great design meter that has needle gauges that show that you have reads from the field. There is also a high as well as a normal setting to adjust sensitivity. includes a fine wire probe that fits on the back of the gauge. If EMF's field levels reach the level of high, flash of red lights will be displayed and a sounder will let that you know it is high levels. It typically costs between PS25.00 or PS35.00.

Additional notes It is sensitive to sudden movements. Any motion will trigger the Red Light coming on as well as the buzzer. It is

it is recommended to hold your hands steady always with it is recommended to keep a steady hand at all times with. In case the battery is depleted when you turn on the device, it can sound as if it is drained.

Moditronic Ramsey

The most expensive EMF tri Field meters available. it's not available for sale and is a very scarce product. However, you are able to locate a less expensive version of the device, that you can make yourself

Kits for sale.

As similar to the Tri Field meter we talked about in the past, this monitors Electrostatic, Magnetic and the ION Sum. However, it does not have the battery test feature but this monitor has some useful features...

There's a row lighting at the very uppermost part of the base. This light is red and indicates the strength of the field. At the center of the meter, there is a rows of

LEDS that lead to the shape of an arch, one that leads towards the left side and the

Other to the left. It also indicates which direction the text is coming from that is being discussed, so it's best to know which direction the text originates from.

The other great feature of this particular meter is its ability to detect people's electrostatic field by placing the Meter at the

base. This will erase your ES measurement, which will affect the meters. If you're located within an area that has some EMF field, it is possible to also cancel it out by using the zero adjust nozzle that is on the base of your unit. This is sometimes a challenge.

Other points The meter is an excellent instrument, however it could become a bit complicated to work when it is time to start the meter it will require you to zeroadjust the sprayer, so that only the two blinking red lights will be on. It can be a bit tricky in some instances.

Full Spectrum Camera

Here's an Camcorder / Camera which can observe the full spectrum. UV UltravioletWhite light and the IR is infrared.

In the night and daytime "an IR light source is needed to see in total darkness"

There are numerous versions of cameras that are full spectrum, Andy of Infraready will tailor the camera to meet your preferences, as well as budget. I suggest visiting www.infraready.co.uk

Chapter 15: Franks Box

The franks box can also be called"ghost box" or "ghost box"

It is a simple radio that scans AM and FM radio wavebands and does not stop on the channel it continues to scan channels from beginning until the end.

The belief is that spirits and ghosts could speak to one another through a device like this In America there have been séances and made it possible for the public to pay "similar to a clairvoyance night" in which people asked questions of the device by the order of turns.

check if they receive an email from family members.

The prices are fairly high in the marketplace at the time, PS50 100

There are a variety of versions of the franks' box by simply searching on ebay, you can find them.

Additional notes Mostly used for spiritual purposes Certain scientific teams make use of these devices, but the information that comes through does not necessarily mean that they are proof of ghosts. It might be a case of pot luck.

GEO Phone

We have this strange appearance device that could look like something from a film called ghostbusters.

It is a vibrating censor. The stronger the vibrating, the more LEDs illuminate. There are some devices that have an sensitivity knob located at the top of the device so you can adjust it to be more sensitive or less so.

The concept is to make use of this as a trigger for investigations. This can be done by using an EVP camera pointed towards the object, or in an EVP session.

The world is silent, you call on your spirits to create an impact, and this

The device will then inform the user if there are any vibrations that are present around the device. Some devices also have the ability to sound, and will alert the user.

The cost varies between PS30 to PS80 based on which model you purchase. Certain models have only audio, while others include leds, while some come with both.

Beam Barriers

A common device that is typically used in locked rooms in the event of the possibility of an entity walking across the hall, through the room and so on.. It is a matter of lining up both devices facing the other at each end of the hall or room If something happens to the beam, the barrier are sounded.

An alarm that sounds loud, alerts you that the beam is breached.

They are quite loud, so loud that they could become irritating if you deliberately struck by you, and it is recommended to place them away from the area you'll be. Additionally, you should have some sort of a video recorder or CCTV camera to monitor the device so that you can prove nobody walks through.

The price is approximately PS5 to PS20

Humidity Meter

The use of humidity meters isn't often seen in paranormal investigations, however it is one of the tools we employ on investigation. The humidity meter is a device that measures the quantity of water droplets present in the air.

It is intended to utilize the device to act as a tool for debunking, as well as a trigger device. (Asking spirits to alter the Meter)

If, for instance, a person on your team receives an ODD MIST photo, that they believe isn't actually their personal breath, then your idea could be to employ this device and calculate the % humidity. If the humidity is greater than 80 percent, the result is

It's very easy to capture the image. Price PS10 PS100

Data Logger

Data loggers are tiny device that resembles the USB flash memory stick. This device is used to monitor and record Temperature and Humidity at the exact in the exact timeframes you set on your laptop. After setting, you are able to remove it from your laptop and put it wherever you want at the desired location. It will then record temperatures and humidity each 10 minutes, or as often.

When you are done, connect the datalogger onto your laptop. Choose the day you would like to see a report as well as to.

It'll be something similar to the one below.

Prices include PS30 PS60 EM PUMP/POD

A em pump, also known as a pod, is a tiny device that emits electro Magnetic fields through the air and surrounding the device. it is believed that spirits and ghosts are fed with energy. Several individuals and teams have reported battery drain from their equipment as well as swore that to be charged. an EM Pump around is designed to save batteries, as well as give spirits the energy needed to accomplish something when they're truly present.

Personally, I think they haven't really done much to help us..

The prices are PS20 to PS60.

Parascope

8 CHANNEL
TRIBO ELECTRIC
FIELD METER

This is an interesting looking gadget that is actually the Electro Static field measurement device. "Not an EMF meter" The device is extremely sensual, and it is able to detect the electro static field of your body.

The idea behind this object is to utilize this object to trigger an object.

The tubes depict the straight of the field and the motion. It is a mixture of colors, including orange, green, red, yellow. This is extremely bright when lighting is off. This is ideal for any camera equipped with

with no night shot.

The gadget requires 4 AAA batteries. It is available by Paranologies

www.paranologies.com

Chapter 16: Shadow Detector

The device that you can use is an laser grid pen or white light. The device should be set up within a space; put an optical grid on top of the device. If a shadow is detected on the laser grid the device will sound an alarm, and light up when you operate the device while the lights are in the room, it will look for shadows "black shadows"

When the lights are off, it will require a light source to make use of the product. If the light source is turned on, just set the item wherever you want, and observe if it is able to be able to detect any shadows.

Price $50

A sound level meter doesn't get utilized that frequently in investigation, but it is utilized by scientists in order for taking base readings of the ambient sound,

We can't even listen to, below 20hz, these devices are able to listen far beyond what we can hear, however you cannot connect headphones to the device or record on any way. All you get is the chart of numbers that range that range from 0 through 100. the user can only see

It is not advisable to have zero readings, since there's always some disturbance.

You can use the meter for your EVP sessions as certain models have back lights which allows you to read figures in dark conditions. This is so that you can ask questions and monitor for the sound to be slowed down following the session.

The question was posed by you.

Price PS7 PS40

Laser Grid

A laser grid is a concept which came into the paranormal field around the year 2010 by TV programs, which were within the paranormal field.

It's it's a Laser pen. It comes with an attachment on the one end, which divides the laser into thousands of tiny dots. is adjustable in dimensions and number via the cap.

It is suggested to do the Camcorder or camera and capture pictures of the grid. You can check if objects appear on the grid. If someone were to wander into the grid, you'd see the green dots appear.. And

You can see the shadows in the grid created by the camera.

Price PS5 PS35

CCTV Equipment

USB DVR

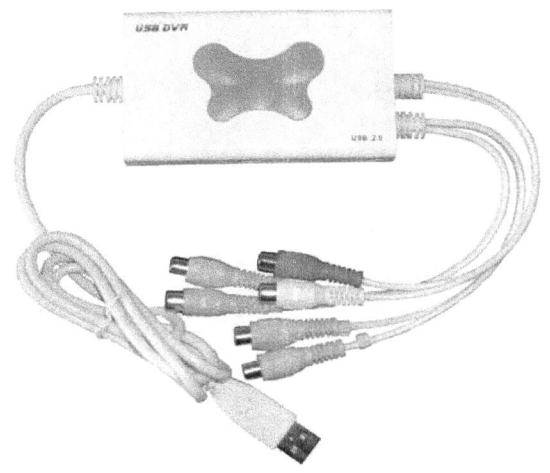

You can purchase either one or four channels of USB DVRS that can be connected to laptops and transforms into a security system. The DVR directly into the USB port of the laptop. connect your CCTV cameras into the sockets in yellow on the DVR Start the software that comes with the DVR then press record.

Illuminators can be purchased as well as all kinds of CCTV cameras

Price PS8 PS60.

Most affordable place to shop is eBay!

Thermal Imager

It's what is the Holy Grail for paranormal investigators it's more of a dream piece of equipment. The thermal imager can determine the temperature of cold and hot

Spots, on areas. They're not created to detect midair temperature variations.

One thing to keep in mind is smaller cameras don't snap pictures. You may purchase a DVR cameras that record. A quick search on ebay for thermal imagers can yield both cameras as well as the DVRS

The Pendulum

A spiritual instrument with a lowcost budget to conduct paranormal research, mostly for teams of spiritualists, you want to keep your hands as bare as you can and

You may ask for individuals willing to help shift the Pendulum,

Inform them to turn the pendulum clockwise for yes or anti clockwise if they don't want to.

Price PS1 PS5

Other Tips to make this an academic experiment, you need to purchase the Jewellery stand to hang chains on and ask the participants to place their hands on the floor of the stand.

This stops the movement created through the pendulum's hold. You should choose an iron stand that will conduct the energy.

3D Full Spectrum Camera (or standard 3D Camera)

However, this type of equipment isn't often used around the world I can see a 3D camera as a valuable instrument for scientific and spiritual research.

investigators as it permits the user to observe what ghostly figures are in the image you can take a picture.

In a regular Camera "non 3d" you are able to always determine the distance from an object, the distance to which something is. A 3D camera can give the user a clear view of what's happening, and can actually assist you to get rid of images that are not as good.

If you'd like purchase a 3D Full Spectrum Contact Andy at www.Infraready.co.uk

Van Der Graaf

It is known as the Van Der graaf has an unorthodox instrument that isn't often employed in research, but it's an enormous EM Pump.

The device produces huge amount of Electrostatic. It is released from the belt through the Metal dome. If you touch the dome, you'd get an unpleasant shock.

2. The reason it is recommended to use this gadget is to fill a space with electrostatic, as well as to shut off

cameras inside the room so that you can see what happens "totally lock the room down, close all doors, and don't go in until you want to turn the machine off"

Another motive is to perform a Van der Graaf symphony. Two people are sitting in each other around the van der graaf two people meeting the dome of metal at the opposite ends, everyone joining hands. You're creating an entire circle that includes that Van der graaf Then, you need to you need someone to get out of the circle and turn the machine off.

It is believed that this can help the spirits influence or do something for your life, but one thing to be aware of is that positive energy causes negative effects on your body. It can make the person feel sick, as if you've been touched, other such.

Wireless EVP

The product is it's a Wireless Mic, and a Receiver, which is plugged into the Laptop's Mic socket. Just place the Mic on the subject you wish to watch it, turn on the receiver connect it to the laptop. Open Audacity "search Google for Audacity download" that is a program for audio that allows you to watch the live stream of the EVP you took from the upstairs room.

Temper Scope

We have a new version of paranologies. It's another stylish and cool design.

This gadget shows the ambient temperature changes in the form of Blue for cold or RED for hot.

The device will serve to trigger objects, thus requesting spirits to stroll past it and so on, in order to determine whether there is any temperatures

Changes, but the best aspect about this is that once again, it's simple to observe the

The darkness! This means that your cameras and other devices are able to see the camera, even when disrupted.

Chapter 17: What Qualities Are Exhibited By Ghost Hunters?

Become an investigator of paranormal phenomena or a ghost hunter, you need to possess the following qualities such as objectivity, patience determination, courage as well as total sincerity. But, believers as well as people who do not believe must possess the ability to put aside their minds long enough in order to be able to assess all information independently. Make sure that you're emotionally prepared to gain a tangible understanding of opposing viewpoints in the event that you discover proof to back this assertion. This is not the only way to go. Ghost hunters today know that the investigation into paranormal phenomenon must be conducted with seriousness, using a sense of respect and prudence. It's not a fun parlor event or a fun-filled party game.

The most effective psychic investigators are those who actively developed patience and trust. A person who is peaceful and mature adds credibility and stability to their investigation. These traits are crucial for dealing with an anxious customer in the midst of stress. Develop the qualities of patience and trust not just to benefit yourself however, for the good of your clients and colleagues. Because of its nature, the realm of the paranormal is one of chaos and uncertainty. As the one that is assigned to sort out the difficult problems and to answer the tough issues, need to be a rock solid source of confidence and stability. Be aware that those who come to you with a need for assistance may be frightened or angry and may not realize they are directing your emotions towards you. Don't take it personally. Also, you may want to explore methods for relaxing your mind and body and focus such as meditation or yoga, including concentration meditation, mindfulness meditation or even breathing meditation. They can assist you to improve your ability to control your emotions that can aid you deal with your clients or being in stressful situations when you are researching.

Maintain a skeptical yet open-minded attitude as you investigate the world of the supernatural. According to scientist Rupert Sheldrake says, "Healthy Skepticism is a key factor in the field of science and encourages inquiry and an enlightened mind. Skeptics who are healthy are open and are interested in the evidence. In contrast, dogmatic skeptics believe that phenomena that appear to be supernatural can't be believed to be true or, at the very least, so inconceivable that they should not receive consideration. Therefore, any evidence supporting these phenomena is likely to be false."

Your credibility as a ghost investigator is dependent on your impartiality. Skeptics and critics say that the majority of ghost hunters are insecure. Ghost hunters are often labeled fantasy-prone personalities--people who like to make things up.

Though the skeptical analysis of ghost hunters might seem to be somewhat skewed however, it is a good reminder of the significance of paranormal investigators who are completely professional and reliable during their job.

The standard operating procedures for your company must include meticulously keeping documents and ensuring that clients are able to fulfill their commitments and privacy while seeking common explanations for everyday events.

Your Essential Equipment List

What are essential items of equipment needed to help you hunt for ghosts?

An extra flashlight as well as batteries. It's not unusual for flashlights to go in the course of an investigation. There are some who believe that supernatural entities trigger these devices to cease working. According to the theory, entities attempt to manifest through taking energy from their surroundings and can often deplete brand new batteries in just a few moments.

A first-aid kit. If you're walking through ancient buildings at night Be prepared with scratches or bumps.

Pencil or notebook. pen. Pens and pencils from the past are crucial in keeping track of the details and the sequence of things.

Watches. Consider investing in a vintage wristwatch that isn't running using batteries. If you can, buy an old-fashioned watch with a secondhand.

Tape recorders. It is a choice of digital or analog. However, it should include an external microphone which is positioned away from the recording device to reduce the amount of static and noise.

Cameras. It may be either a film or a digital camera. It should come with a flash to ensure that it is possible to utilize it, or not. Bring extra camera batteries. (For specific information regarding camera equipment, accessories and how to use them, read the chapter on 76.)

An electromagnetic frequency (EMF) meter. This latest tool to measure ghosts analyzes the electromagnetic field within the region. (For specific information regarding EMF meters, their uses and the best place to find one, read Chapter 80.)

Cell phones are a must. It isn't always a good idea when you're in a hot spot that's not normal, however, you should have one just in case you have to contact others on the team or contact for assistance. Do not venture out in a group or not telling anyone who else you know where your group will be, and the time you'll plan to return.

Other non-essential, cheap gadgets that are low-tech and easy to add to your collection of ghost hunting tools might include:

A match and candles, or a lantern made of kerosene. They are an excellent alternative in the event that your light bulb goes out.

A pendulum. This is a traditional method to communicate with spirit.

Dowsing rods. They can be used similar ways to an EMF measurer.

Strings of black and rubber. The two can be attached to entry points in order to identify if anyone is in or out of the location without your knowing.

A detector for magnetic anomalies to determine the existence of magnetic field anomalies which may signal the existence abnormal paranormal activity.

Yardsticks or tape measures are used to gauge any object that appears to be moving from its previous position.

An outline of the site for you to familiarize yourself and others with the layout of the area.

The most crucial things you should add to the investigation are your sense of humor, ability to discern and investigate along with a friend. Don't venture out without a partner; you might get injured or stranded somewhere.

Chapter 18: Keeping Accurate Records

Notes are essential to record any strange phenomena, regardless of whether there is a video camera recording the research. Notes are an excellent means of recording vital details. However, the camera won't capture every angle in one go but it can't be aware of what you've recently experienced on a personal level, such as an impression, a frozen spot or ghostly touching. Writing down the reactions you have to events which occur will help trace the event in the future.

These are a few things you should be aware of while you write notes and record the results of your study:

Note down anything you believe is important. Write down any explanations you could have. In the case of, say, you notice a decrease in temperature, one possible plausible explanation could be a weakly insulation in the room or a pending changing in the weather.

Then, you can eliminate any events or anomalies that appear suspicious, and might have common explanations.

Make a list of the other items by category, and according to importance to make sure you are clear on your thoughts as well as to assist you in organizing your list in order.

Don't discard less significant facts. Instead, you should move them toward the back of your report and be aware of the possibility that their significance could alter as you investigate.

Do not ignore the power of random chance. A majority of research involves aspects of coincidence or randomness.

If you are analyzing your data, look for significant correlations and probabilities to the data in order to reduce the amount of speculation that you make in your assessments and conclusion. Examining the evidence with care that you have gathered from both your experience and also from electronic recordings of voice phenomena and Digital video recording (DVRs) as well as digital thermometers can help you to make an informed decision that will be able to stand criticism from critics and disbelievers.

Make a note of your investigation. They are known by various names like the paranormal investigation logbook, the paranormal investigator's logbook and the paranormal the vigil log. No matter what they're called they help to maintain a record of crucial research data as well as serve as references in the event that something unusual occurs. The notebooks also include the records of investigators on the apparatus used as well as the readings taken of the equipment.

An ideal logbook will have room to write:

Temperature, weather conditions, barometric pressure

EMF field activation

The moon's phase

Sunspot activity

Equipment checklist

Equipment utilized in particular studies, and base measurements

Remarkable investigative events

Personal experiences that are ambiguous

Contact details for individuals, which include emergency contact details, medication and medical details

Even the most basic logs ought to have a space for the investigator's thoughts, experiences and possible paranormal events are recorded. When an investigator's hair gets pulled back, or if she smells roses, receives an impression of hearing or sees ghosts, they must be recorded on the paper in order for comparing information between locations and investigators.

Your Paranormal Self-Education

If you choose to work as a paranormal researcher, whether as a pastime or an occupation, it is essential build up a library of reference material and educate yourself on the various types of supernatural phenomena and hauntings. Online sources and book stores like Amazon.com offer these materials and books, magazines and web sites accessible to all.

If you're an inquirer and open-minded mindset and an open mind, you'll have a thrilling experience to come. There's plenty to know and a lot to discover. Furthermore, what you gain will impact how you think about the world, your own life, and others who surround you.

Where should you start? A book can be an excellent, easy way to get started.

The books on occult from British writer Colin Wilson are very thorough and in-depth. Mysteries, The Occult, and Poltergeist are highly recommended.

D. Scott Rogo's Welcoming Silence: An Investigation of Psychological Phenomena as well as the Survival of Death and Haunted House Handbook provide a thorough overview of the topic.

Loyd Auerbach's ESP, Hauntings and Poltergeists is another great work that provides a comprehensive overall overview of.

When you are reading books about the paranormal, be sure to keep a piece of paper and a pen close by to make notes about the ideas and concepts you are interested in or want to explore further.

While you are able to conduct studies via the Internet but make sure that websites you visit are credible and are run by professionals with an extensive background respect, understanding, and a long history in the community of paranormal investigators. Make sure you know which websites have a history of trustworthiness and those that have existed for several years and are proving their worth. The Atlantic Paranormal Society (TAPS) website (www.the-atlantic-paranormal-society.com) has a great deal of information, as does Troy Taylor's (www.prairieghosts.com/abtauthor.html)

and The Rhode Island Paranormal Research Group's (T.R.I.P.R.G. ; www.triprg.com/index1.htm).

While reading and researching can help paranormal investigators prepare for the potential of ghost hunting, attending real-world classes will enable you to understand the nuances and methods. These classes are useful in studying the technical aspects of business like how to manage an EMF gauge and the best way to conduct EVP investigations. EVP (electronic voice phenomenon or recorded sounds that look like voice but aren't recorded intentionally voice recordings) investigations.

Every class you attend should include the following details:

Find haunted locations

What can you do to study the history of the site

How do you interview an eyewitness

How can you construct an equipment for ghost hunting

How do you take a recording of EVPs

What is the best way to utilize EMF meters and thermometers digital

What is the best way to utilize an electronic camera for investigative

What is the best way to create a team or paranormal group

These details should be considered when you enroll in a home-study class, online course, or in a continuing education facility. You should sign up after checking through the credentials of teachers and the institutions.

It is important to check the quality of every class, especially Internet classes. If the standard of the class or the school is not up to par, you will be sure to get feedback from other students.

If you reside in Connecticut, Rhode Island, or Massachusetts there is a chance that you are near enough to drive by The Atlantic Paranormal Society (TAPS)'s day-long seminars and talks. TAPS is the group which is the subject of Syfy Channel's Ghost Hunters TV show. While the price of TAPS's workshops is usually inexpensive ($40 for one-day seminars) They do, however, have a very high demand for their workshops.

Classes online vary greatly in price. The classes that cost $100 can be considered to be at the top price point. Flamel College (www.flamelcollege.org) offers a paranormal investigator certification for $99. This includes an EMF measurement. Universal Class (www.universalclass.com) has a very reasonably priced ($20) online class for beginning investigators. After certification, it's only $45.

Fiona Broome, the founder of Hollow Hill (www.hollowhill.com), a ghost hunters' website, offers classes in different levels so students can take classes appropriate to their situation. The classes are available via CDs.

A conference might be more than what you're searching for. There are ghost hunting groups that hold annual retreats that last for several days, including Ghost tours, workshops or paranormal research, as well as media-related presentation. Search for "ghost hunter conference" into the Internet search engine, and check what results appear.

Chapter 19: Building And Organizing A Team

A new investigator might decide to invite a handful of like-minded acquaintances to create the paranormal community. Establish a set of rules and establish a procedure to conduct investigations as early as possible. It is easier to conduct investigations if all members of the group are aware of the fundamental theories that underlie paranormal oddities and has completed some of the suggested readings.

In most cases, the group breaks down into groups of two and then they travel to different places that must be explored. Combine investigators whose styles have a similarity and their capabilities complement each other. The kind of relationship that this type of pairing creates is ideal as a lot more is possible by ensuring that the investigators' personalities work well together. It is not a good idea to pair individuals who are on one and argue about the procedures. Leaders of teams who must handle this type of situation are often frustrated working with issues that are human as opposed to paranormal ones. The passion and enthusiasm of investigators to the case could affect the result and drastically alter the outcome of the case So, be sure to select members that are capable of putting their egos aside and collaborate well in tandem with other team members.

With the interest in investigating the paranormal increases, many teams are flooded by new members' requests. This might seem like a great option, but remember to examine and screen the new members prior to inviting new members as member of your group. The profession of paranormal investigation is not an option for everyone. It is a unique combination of characteristics (objectivity perseverance, focus, and strength, to mention only a handful) and the desire for exploration as well as a constant thirst for knowledge and a responsible and mature attitude to this field. Selecting members with care is just crucial as is training the right ones, so create a questionnaire to filter out those who are thrill seekers, as well as those who are reckless or unstable. The type of questions you should ask to help get there is up to the particular group that you are in however, each application must contain questions regarding the potential members' education, employment and educational background, as well as hypothetical scenarios that will test their common sense.

Be sure that the individuals you gather with are able to can communicate effectively and freely share details. If you're forced to pull off the data or repeatedly ask them to clarify the information, odds are they'll omit crucial details while working as well as during the process of reviewing evidence and so on. People who are drawn to the supernatural certainly follow a different beat and it's no reason they aren't discussing the everyday daily business associated with their other interesting projects? But, if the investigators don't have the ability to effectively communicate, they will not achieve their goals or appreciate their investigations as they would otherwise or even delay the investigations.

Incorporating an Established Paranormal Research GroupSometimes the toughest aspect of the hunt is finding other people to train or work with.

A membership in a reputable group is the most effective option to gain the best instruction and develop the capabilities you'll need to be an investigator in the paranormal field. Look for paranormal groups which meet frequently within your local area. Look for people with a good reputation for being psychics or investigators of the paranormal. Also, you can utilize the Internet. Search for the city or location and include the phrase "ghost hunters." You could find that there's an established group in the area.

If you spot a team that you're keen to join make contact or write an email to make yourself known. Make the time to get together and determine if you could plan an investigation into ghosts. The majority of people working who work in the field of paranormal are extremely friendly. They're in task of aiding others struggling, typically on their own and are therefore most likely to accept friendly gestures.

The majority of paranormal groups who conduct investigation have forms which new members are required to complete.

The purpose of this is to make certain that you are aware of the obligations as well as the potential dangers and concerns regarding the law that are involved with the field of paranormal investigations. The form protects you from any legal responsibility should something occur to you during the course of your investigation. Additionally, you will be informed about the procedures of the organization as well as the methods used to conduct an investigation. You are likely to be put on probation till you have completed the course. This will ensure you are aware of all possible implications of your actions in the event of an unexpected incident.

The groups actively seek for people who have mental issues as well as those who use substances or alcohol. Smoking cigarettes is not permitted when conducting investigations, for a number of reasons. Smoking can pose an ablaze hazard within old constructions, and smoke may be confused with ghostly fog or mists.

They are also taught to maintain their faith private. The inevitable thing is that individuals who are conducting an investigation might be able to start discussing questions about the afterlife, and also the issue of what happens after the death. The discussion of this sort is appropriate, however if it becomes the discussion of a person's faith, it may cause discord and a lack of unity within the group.

An effective organization must provide you with and instruct your in the latest techniques of trade in the way they're used today. There may be a particular desire for a specific device, like the dowsing rod or a digital camera. If you notice an area that you excel at something, then you must build your knowledge in the area and the team will be happy the presence of someone competent and enthusiastic. There are no two researchers alike, and each person's skills will differ.

An eloquent manner of speaking and ability to observe are crucial for every paranormal investigator. If you're able to stay objective and remain aware of the world around you, you can be a valuable member of any organization that you are a part of. If you are blessed with abilities to sense, you are able to improve your ability to sense and be sensitive in this area. An on-the-job learning in this field occurs due to the results you get from the results of an examination.

In the beginning, you'll likely be working with an experienced detective to collect eyewitness reports. Pay attention to the kinds of questions addressed. Equally important, take note of the manner in which they are addressed. Certain organizations conduct interviews with potential clients in order to determine whether a complete investigation is necessary. A team member with experience examines the data provided. An inspection of the premises can be scheduled during this period too. Certain groups invite psychics accompanying them to their initial interviews in order to find out if any paranormal phenomenon can be identified in particular when the person who has contacted them mentions the possibility of some kind of poltergeist, or other harmful act that could compromise the safety and well-being of the people who live or work at the location. Particularly, when there are children present in the area. All efforts must be put in to expedite the process in cases where the health of children is on the line.

A WORD OF CAUTION

The paranormal investigations that are often advertised can be scams. The main goal of these groups is to scare the customer to believe that certain objects within their homes are cursed or are possessed, and should be destroyed immediately. The items they are looking for are typically precious antiques, or valuable items which are later traded or pawned.

Chapter 20: Follow Strict Protocols To Protect Credibility

Many organizations are implementing strict procedures to hunt ghosts. It is rare to find a group today that completely ignores the scientific approach in favor of the barging-around-an-old-house approach of yesteryear. Organizations that make this mistake are soon without customers and are confronted with real problems with credibility.

The scientific method is where investigators try to find and analyze the evidence, just declaring the situation to be as supernatural after all other explanations are discarded. This is sometimes in conflict with investigations that do not aim to debunk or reopen the mysteries, but rather to resolve the mystery. There are a few variations between groups However, those looking for concrete evidence of hauntings should be able to follow the same guidelines in order in order to accomplish their goals. Examples:

They are given permission to access the website, and then they have to clear it through the organization or person is responsible for access.

The investigators are together. Investigators work together so that nobody is left alone.

The strictest records are maintained of the equipment being used, and the electronic equipment is inspected for accuracy prior to being put into the field in order to guarantee its security.

The occurrence that was described is examined for repeatability using natural ways.

The information is meticulously examined and scrutinized in order to disprove the claims.

The evidence that can't be disproved is archived properly and kept.

The aim is to collect solid, reliable evidence for existence after death, messages that have gone through, the phenomenon of poltergeists and even a malevolent ghostly presence. If evidence proves to be uncertain, it's dismissed. The practice can cause conflict within groups. Members may claim that evidence is reliable while other members believe that it's not. A lot of groups organize sessions for evidence where members are able to examine the evidence and decide on whether or not they want to preserve it.

Scientific methodology is an extremely difficult discipline to master. Some investigators do not think it's a good practice, particularly in the case of focusing on gathering information rather than supporting the individuals that are in distress.

The best ghost hunter are those who don't forget their motivation for entering the field in the first instance--just to aid others. If a lot of evidence has been collected on a case, but families have been evicted from their house and the investigation does not end with a positive solution.

The most intriguing experiences occur when an investigator experiences a personal experience of a supernatural event. However, if the incidents aren't confirmed by tangible evidence such as an image or recording and aren't taken as evidence of any kind even though a third party witnessed the event. Data should be obtained by using a scientific approach:

1. The question should be defined. For a paranormal investigation, this may be something like "What is causing the unusual events as detailed by this client?"

2. Find information and sources.

3. Create an hypotheses.

4. Make experiments and record information. You'll require a camera and an audio recorder an electronic watch and a notepad, to accomplish this.

5. Analyze data.

6. Analyze data and draw conclusions to serve as a beginning place for the development of a new hypothesis.

7. Create the results.

8. Always retest.

Following the Scientific Method

The science behind paranormal research could help to end those false perceptions of investigators being gullible and unscientific. In the end, ghost hunters are beginning to gain credibility and getting taken more seriously. There are some skeptical people who believe that the ghost hunters' claims are fake science, but as the evidence builds, minds are opening.

In order for the field to earn respect and credibility, researchers are aware of two things. The first is to eliminate the evidence which could be based on an explanation that is normal. In addition, they must adhere to the scientific method in their research.

A researcher who employs the scientific method should be at the same time open and skeptical. Any phenomenon should be scrutinized. To determine the root of the issue, the investigator will need to ask questions that are based on the method of science:

The reason for the incident?

Are there any natural source of the problem?

Does this happen in connection with another cause?

Have you identified connections between your observations and other events? have witnessed?

Are other researchers coming to similar conclusion?

What's your theory? Do you think it is in line with colleagues' hypothesis or is it a new idea?

What are you going to do to determine the validity of your idea?

Chapter 21: Instinct Versus Intellect

Some skeptical individuals dismiss the entire investigation into the paranormal in a binary question of intuition versus intelligence. But, it is important to not consider intellect and intuition as opposing one another. When you conduct your research and studies into the paranormal it is likely that you rely on both.

Your ability to comprehend and analyze can play an important role in the investigation. It is important to search to find a plausible explanation for every observed or documented phenomena before deciding that an phenomenon is purely supernatural in its origin. In most instances, it is possible to discover a common explanation if you look at the evidence in depth. Since the 18th century in the nineteenth century, it was the Society for Psychical Research (SPR) was trying to disprove the phenomenon or explain it using the use of natural methods. The present-day investigators have taken this method of looking at the paranormal further. It's a great approach to follow.

However, listening to your gut is equally important. Your instincts can inform you that something could pose a risk or point you towards the right place or location in which your research can yield results. It is important to maintain a equilibrium between intuition and intellect.

If you're a paranormal researcher, it is essential to improve your ability to observe at an unimaginable level. Once you've learned how to operate the equipment and have mastered the numerous tips and tricks for successful fieldwork, you must develop the abilities that allow you to look at your surroundings with a sharp eyes. In order to do that be able to evaluate the area in a neutral manner. Find a way to let go of any emotions and get rid of any assumptions you make regarding a place or a situation. The first step is to look at the factual information. You can get a report of strange incidents from the customer, after which you can make your own observations and conclusions about those instances.

If you take the time to investigate for long enough, you'll come across a situation that can't be explained using any natural laws or disproved with a common sense explanation. In this case it is crucial to remain in a clear and alert the mind. It is easy to say however, it is difficult to implement. If the mind of a human being is faced with a situation it is unable to rapidly categorize, or easily comprehend and it is prone to slow down or spiral into chaos. The heart could pound, and your mind may become scattered or confusing.

What can you do to deal when you're experiencing these feelings? It's not an easy one. Each person is different in handling anxiety and fears. If you're a complete skeptical person, it could be that you are completely shut out and refuse to think about or accept what you're witnessing. However If you've got an inclination to remain open and open-minded, you'll be equipped to deal with the issue. If you're in any way it is best to work in tandem with another person and employ technologies to keep an impartial document of the situation. Be sure to conduct yourself with an appearance as professional as possible, considering the circumstance. Ghost hunting can be subject to criticism and ridicule and scrutiny, therefore a thorough research is essential.

www.ingramcontent.com/pod-product-compliance
Lightning Source LLC
Chambersburg PA
CBHW071441080526
44587CB00014B/1945